The UNFORGETTABLE TREE

KEN KLEIN

MidPoint Trade Books, Inc.

All biblical quotes are from the King James Bible

ISBN
978-09982985-0-4 (Paperback)
978-09982985-1-1 (eBook)

1. Religion, Biblical Studies

Dreams have played a significant role in the direction of history and many times have altered the course of history. This book is not just another piece of literature. It is a supernatural doorway to a real spiritual reality with God through the visitation of Angels.

ACKNOWLEDGMENT

ഇം∙ളൂ

This remarkable lost knowledge has been in front of the world, but covered over by religious tradition for seventeen centuries.

For all who hold to the name of Jesus/Yeshua may you find the revelation life changing and strengthening to stand before him without fear against that Day.

Thank you to Dr. Ernest Martin for his guidance.

> "Now thanks be unto God, which always causeth us to triumph in Christ, and maketh manifest the savor of his knowledge by us in every place"
>
> **(2 Cor. 2:14)**

TESTIMONIALS FOR THE UNFORGETTABLE TREE

Pastor Gary Van Landingham

Ken mines resources, both historical as well as contemporary, to discover and communicate wisdom, insights and very important facts than can change human history.

Jerry McMillum –
CEO 4 Cast Broadcasting Corp
"The Unforgettable Tree"

I was fortunate enough to have read "The Unforgettable Tree" by Author Ken Klein. First I will say, I have followed this author for many years and his films as well as other publications. This book will open your eyes and hearts to what Christ really did that goes far beyond what we have learned in traditional Church curriculum. This latest book literally pulls you into the story of the ride into Jerusalem on a donkey by Christ himself by the temple on Passover holiday all the way to the crucifixion and how much more He did in that Historical event than we have been taught. The story once it is understood in its power packed verbiage which is typical of a very insightful, gifted and spiritual writer such as Ken Klein is literally enough to set you free from the traditional Christian's perspective.

No longer do you need to be beating yourself up over past, present and future sins committed, regardless of what you have been taught. Quit flogging yourselves and know what Christ meant when he said; I came so that you may have life and have it more abundantly.

What an eye opener.

This is a book that has to be read for those seeking true freedom and a mind that is not filled with wardens of the mind that beat you up every time you commit the smallest of sins. Jesus brings on a whole new and powerful element to Christianity that has never been deciphered through scripture until now.

Do yourself and loved ones a favor and read this book and learn to live free and confident in who Jesus is and what He really accomplished on the tree for us. You will be glad you did and you will be set free for life. No shame, No guilt. It melts all that away.

—Jerry Mc Mullan

Dr. Ken Beros

I am a 67 year old dentist whose hobby has been studying the Hebrew and Greek of the Bible for over 40 years. Ken Klein University and now his new book "The Unforgettable Tree" just blew me away! Ken's knowledge of ancient history is outstanding. And you don't have to be a Bible scholar to understand it. Ken reveals secret knowledge hidden in God's Word. And he makes it easy to understand even for the Bible novice. Thanks, Ken! Great job!

Dr. Cyndi Romine
Ken! Wonderful!!

Ken Klein has done it again. This is an amazing read of thought and research. A must read.

Only with in depth thinking and research would this truth have come into our sight. It is a book that makes you stop and rethink what you think and how you pray.

Prayer is our glue that holds us to the Righteous One and this new insight will bring you to your knees in a new way.

Again, a must read.

Editor at FriesenPress

Tradition, the author tells us, is the enemy of truth, and what Ken Klein has pieced together after forty- six years of biblical study is nothing short of the truth behind the Crucifixion—the where, the how, and the why of the most important event in Christian history.

According to Klein, all three of these aspects of the event have been obscured by the Christian tradition set in place by Emperor Constantine in the fourth century BCE. It is Klein's contention that Jesus died not on a Roman cross at Golgotha at all, but rather hung from a tree, and not just any tree.

It is a shocking assertion to be sure, but one supported by reasoned scholarship and backed up by the excellent work of historian and theologian Ernest L. Martin (1932–2002). It is a compelling read, and for all its scholarship, manages to remain remarkably accessible. That it is capable of finding a receptive audience among open-minded Christian is beyond question.

TABLE OF CONTENTS

৽ঌ

Preface

ഗ⊶⊰

Seventeen hundred years ago, monumental change took place which has continued to influence the world to this day.

The decisions and determinations that brought about those changes came in the fourth century AD during the reign of Emperor Constantine the Great. By the sheer power of his personality, he transformed the entire pagan Roman Empire into his own Christian Empire.

In his quest to rule, he used Christianity as a means to consolidate his empire. The main thrust of his tactics was in the transformation of an illegal Christian religion into a mandated legitimized one. What had formerly been an outlawed religious belief Constantine made safe. It was now fashionable to be a Christian. The removal of the stigma and the gigantic reversal had tremendous implications. The sea change transformed the world in ways that are not fully appreciated or recognized today.

As a result of his success the emperor ultimately determined the content of what would be commonly accepted as the Bible.

He presided over which books would be included in the canon. He would deter- mine what would properly be consider the Sabbath (Sunday). Many of the Church's current doctrines were decided at his Council of Nicaea.

He and his mother, Helena, determined where Jesus died was buried and rose again (at the Church of the Holy Sepulchre).

And finally, and most significantly, he was responsible for the adoption of the symbol that would hence- forth serve as the very brand of the Christian faith: the pagan Roman cross. But what was hailed as his greatest achievement—the legalization of Christianity— has morphed into the shackles that bind the world in religious traditionalism.

Constantine the Great was arguably the most powerful man in the world. As emperor, he had the power of life and death, but he was a pitiful figure. He could not trust anyone, including his wife and son, both of whom he had murdered shortly after the Council of Nicaea.

If you had to sit in judgment of this man would you consider him an instrument of God or a puppet of Lucifer?

Introduction

୨୦୶

O ver the course of time there is an evolution to the dynamic of history. Yet while many things change, there are some issues of life that remain the same. They are static.

One of those remaining issues is something deep within the heart of man, and it is eloquently written in the book of Ecclesiastes.

> "He hath made everything beautiful in his
> time: also he hath set the world in their heart,
> so that no man can find out the work that God
> maketh from the beginning to the end"
>
> **(Eccl. 3:11)**
> **[NB unless otherwise noted, all scripture is
> drawn from the King James Version]**

Every man and every woman contemplates this great mystery and at some point feels that there must be something more to life than a temporary mortal existence. Yet an answer, a *satisfying* explanation, remains out of reach. Meanwhile, lurking nearby the vacuum of emptiness, there is the presence of a grave danger.

As the gnawing need to know strains the reach of the human soul, a vanishing point is reached. It is at that critical juncture where the countless religions of the world stand prepared ready to fill the void.

The unwary and ill-advised soul should take heed. The perilous danger and stark reality is that religions of the world are fraught with myths, legends, superstitions, false histories, and debatable doctrines and dogmas. Such contrived concoctions find their way into vulnerable and inquisitive minds.

Even the Christian religions are fraught with this very problem.

One only has to look at the confusion and foolish- ness of the myriad of sects, denominations, religious orders and the countless and contradictory doctrines of Christendom to see that God is either terribly delusional or there is corporate confusion.

How can there be an escape from the malignant forces pervading the air, forces which inevitably find a way into the minds of men? All have been infected.

Nevertheless, if wisdom is searched, there comes a realization, namely that all have fallen prey to colossal deceit. If the awakening shines light on the mind garden planted with a variety of twisted lies, an uprooting may take place. In this there is hope.

But as the sun dawns on the promising new day, it must also be preceded with a brave and honest evaluation of that which is considered sacred.

Religious traditionalism is, without doubt, the enemy of truth. And we must beware, for it dies hard. Yet, to our good fortune, there is a great light at the end of the long dark tunnel, and that light shines forth in *the unforgettable tree.*

—

Finally, before proceeding, I would like to add a personal note here. There will be many people who wish to discredit this work simply because it uses the Greek *Jesus*, rather than the Hebrew *Yeshua.*

The reason I do this is not to disparage the use of the name Yeshua but rather to personally identify with the Lord as he was treated by the Jews. He was dealt with *outside* the camp—as you will see. He was regarded by them as a Gentile.

Personally I prefer to suffer with him outside the camp in his humiliation as he was considered by the Jews. Since I am a Jew myself, it would be reasonable and logical for me to use his Hebrew name, Yeshua, and not inappropriate either, but I rather use his Gentile name and choose to identify with him in this way.

"Let us go forth therefore unto him without the camp, bearing his reproach"

(Heb. 13:13)

What can be more humiliating than to be an excommunicated Jew treated as a Gentile by his own people?

To me he is Jesus, to others he is Yeshua. He is the same regardless, and I respect that.

Chapter 1

THE BUZZ

ॐ

I f you weren't there you wouldn't have believed it. Who could have? Nothing like this had ever happened before.

As the news spread from village to village, it didn't take long for the whole of Galilee region to be swept up in the fervor. By the time it spread to the village of Capernaum, even the busy fishermen around the sea had become aware of the supernatural event. Galilee was aflame with news that the promised Messiah of Israel had been found and was heading their way.

The news was sensational. A miraculous event had taken place. A voice had been heard from the sky above, and a great light in the bodily form of a dove had descended upon Jesus of Nazareth.[1] What did it mean?

This was astonishing information, and it spread like wild fire throughout the region. But unless you had been there to experience the event firsthand, it would have been hard to accept wholeheartedly.

Supernatural experiences are far removed from the day to day humdrum effects of the present world. This is why human beings are normally unable to warm to the idea of a world beyond the physical. The overwhelming bias of the present negates the consideration of something beyond. Even the suggestion of a world beyond is far too foreign. After all, the here and now is home base. It is a fact of life, therefore, that there is a natural default and reset to the temporal. Even when there is a modicum of interest, the physical mortal existence swallows up the spiritual.

Furthermore, once a person is tapped with any experiential knowledge of the dimension beyond, relating the spiritual experience to another person is a difficult chore and a stressful circumstance. The spiritual dimension and the physical world are simply incompatible. They do not co-exist peacefully. When they encounter each other, it is as though two planets are in collision. It can be a bitter pill, a difficult inter- action to say the least.

The sensational news that came to Galilee was beyond the scope of normal day to day experience, and to those of the region was earth shaking. And yet it was somewhat credible because for hundreds of years it had been foretold by their prophets that a day like this was coming. The people had been set up and prepared.

It wasn't just John, though. Other witnesses were saying the same thing and testifying that they too had heard a powerful voice and had seen the amazing light come down. Was this the news that all Israel had been waiting for?

The Hebrew people had long heard of the prophesies about a Messiah who would come and restore the kingdom of David. They were cautiously optimistic, but after centuries of waiting, they were not sure what to expect.

Would they too see confirming signs that this was he? They wanted proof. They needed to see. Nonetheless, with guarded hope, they were primed.

It was common knowledge the prophecies had fore- told that a star[2] would rise out of Jacob, and he would come to restore the kingdom of David. It was because of the prophecies that there was a hope and expectancy attending the minds of the people.

It appeared this was a possibility, perhaps the very reality they had been waiting for. After hearing John speak, the people were anxious, but they had no clue as to the magnitude of the supernatural intrusion which was about to break on them.

It wasn't difficult, though, to convince Andrew and his brother Simon that Jesus was the one spoken of in prophesy. They didn't need signs and wonders; they immediately began to follow him. Then there was the third: Nathanael.

Perhaps it was his mannerism or his countenance, but Nathanael had a nature about him that Jesus could see into as he observed him standing under the fig tree. What a perfect location in which to be discovered, under a fig tree.[3]

From the outset, little thought was given to the significance of the fig tree. It was just an another tree. There were many fig trees, but the significance of the fig tree would take on tremendous physical, metaphorical and symbolic meaning.

After his introduction, Nathanael disappeared from any prominence in the story. He was brought forward, but soon thereafter disappears from sight. There are few superstars in God's economy, and Nathanael becomes conspicuously absent.

He blends in and is just a peripheral character. He was just an average normal guy same as most people. Everyone can relate with Nathanael, and he represents the bystander. In a manner of speaking, we are all observers, waiting to be discovered under that fig tree. We are all Nathanael in the story.

Jesus had an extraordinary ability. He possessed a kind of spiritually penetrating vision. His supernatural gifting manifested continuously, over and over again. He could see into the spirit realm, whether into time, space, matter, angels, demons, people, or events. He could see with far-reaching spiritual clarity. Jesus had faraway eyes.

When he spoke, he spoke from the perspective of his gifting. There was a depth of perception, and when he spoke, he seemed to be speaking from another dimension. A spiritual word would come forth from him. It was continuous and evident throughout his presence on the Earth. No doubt the source of the gifting was the light that had come down upon him. Christ could see well beyond the human condition of the frozen physical realm. In fact, he could see into infinity. He could see into the fluid spiritual dimension.

At first Nathanael was seen at a distance, standing under the fig tree. The fact that he was seen under a fig tree appears at first inconsequential. Nevertheless, Nathanael's calling along with the introduction of the fig tree had deep symbolic—and most importantly *spiritual*—importance. It would represent the context for a powerful and penetrating message.

As far as Nathanael's outer appearance was concerned, he could hardly be distinguished from the other simple fishermen who frequented the docks. There was something about Nathanael that was unique, and Jesus standing at a distance with his spiritual depth of vision saw it. The face to face encounter between Jesus and Nathanael is captured in the gospel of John.

> "Jesus saw Nathanael coming to him, and saith of him, behold an Israelite indeed, in whom is no guile!"
>
> **(John 1:47)**

Nathanael and the people from the north were far different then the pretentious and aloof city dwellers of Jerusalem. They were especially far removed from the know-it-all intellectuals of the priestly class who also dwelt in the big city. Jesus sought out the simple teachable and trainable people of Galilee, and Nathanael was one who stood out to him.

There was a simplicity to Nathanael, an upright, straight-forward honesty. Nathanael was a teach- able man. He could be trained. These traits made him a candidate to be one of the select group of the twelve disciples.

When Nathanael inquired how Jesus had already known him, he was told that he had seen him under the fig tree.

The fact that he was being observed by Jesus—the present hope of the promised Messiah—was an over- whelming thought to the simple fisherman.

> "Nathanael answered and saith unto him, Rabbi, thou art the Son of God; thou art the King of Israel"
>
> **(John 1:49)**

And in light of how little he knew of Jesus, this was an extraordinary response. Nevertheless, Nathanael was completely taken by the possibility that he was being singled out. The idea that he might be a candidate for some divine purpose by the Messiah of Israel was beyond belief. His emotions took over.

"Jesus answered and said unto him, Because
I said unto thee, I saw thee under the fig tree,
believest thou? thou shalt see greater things
than these"

(John 1:50)

What a loaded statement! Only time would reveal the extraordinary reality of the promise.

It was at the very beginning when Jesus would dis- close to him something which had never been promised before—not to any man. He was promised that he would see heaven open and the angels of God ascending and descending on the Son of Man.

What exactly did this mean? It was a shocking promise. The idea of the promise would haunt him from time to time. It was a promise of something beyond this world, a transcendental revelation, a life changing potential.

But the spiritual realm is beyond reach of human cognition. This is why it is so lightly regarded by human beings. The spiritual dimension for mortals is far removed from human credulity. Men and women are focused on the material here-and-now world, not the realm of the spirit.

The human mind is profoundly conditioned by the present physical world. Something such as the promise made to Nathanael was so beyond his experience that his preoccupation with the present material realm made the promise seem surreal. It was impossible to grasp.

Such is the spiritually impoverished state of the human race. It is unfortunate because the present physical world is transitory while the spiritual realm is eternal.

And yet, to transition from the physical to spiritual reality, there is need of change; a transformation must take place. In the short term, for Nathanael, what was to happen over the next three years would prepare him for the heavenly promise.

There was need for a change, an arch of change. The existential promise would, however, have to take a back seat to the more immediate need.

For him to encounter and reach the promise, it would require a process. Nathanael had to be prepared for the ultimate reality. He would have to undergo a transformation and reversal of his earthly mind's programming. What was in store over the next three years would, out of necessity, transform his thinking.

For the time being, the ultimate promise for the supernatural revelation of angels ascending and descending would be pushed to the back of his mind. He would have to wait and undergo a spiritual surgery.

Chapter 2

CONFRONTATION
WITH THE ADVERSARY

๛๏๛

W hen Albert Einstein discovered the theory of relativity, he brought starlight to earth.

Starlight is nuclear. In like manner, the star of David had come down to earth, and Nathanael was about to experience the implications. He was about to be lit up by a spiritual bomb that would obliterate his mortal thinking. What was about to take place could not have been anticipated. It came out of left field. No one, not even Nathanael, was prepared for what was about to happen.

The transformation from the programming of the natural mind to the programming of a spiritual mind requires a spiritual process. The process would not be painful in the physical sense, but it certainly was going to overthrow his rational mind. The process was about to begin.

What was to take place was a myriad of events that would change the very wiring of his mental circuitry. God was about to blow his mind. All temporal thinking was to be obliterated. It was to be overshadowed by a completely new way of thinking.

The current complexion of his mind was contrary to spirituality and would require a massive transformation. The process would challenge and place every category and every definition into question. Everything was put on the operating table. Every mental sequence was to be redefined.

The supernatural promise of angels ascending and descending would be placed in suspension. The process would take precedence. The transcendental idea of seeing angels descending and ascending on the Son of Man was out of reach and off in the distance. And though it was a promise, a planted seed, it receded and left the conscious attention of his mental gaze.

Initially, there would come a myriad of supernatural and miraculous events, which in all of human history had never occurred. The events would pave the way. The revolution of the mind had been prepared and was at hand. All of his preconceived thinking was to be dismantled, and it would change him forever.

Before his very eyes, he was to see astonishing things. To the human mind they were incomprehensible. The very laws and rules of the physical world were interrupted. It was as though things were being turned upside down.

Thousands were fed from seemingly nothing. How could this be? It happened more than once, just to underscore the reality. Then multitudes of people were healed from debilitating diseases. Lame people would walk; some for the first time. Blind people regained their sight. The most dreaded disease of leprosy was arrested and lepers were cured instantly. Water was turned into wine. The laws of nature suspended as Jesus walked on water. These astonishing momentous events were Nathanael's experience. What a curriculum! Nathanael had been immersed in the school of the supernatural.

But since those days, two thousand years have passed, and now it's just history, and second hand knowledge. However, for Nathanael it was real; it was here and now, and it was happening.

On and on, event after event bombarded his human mind. His earthly sensibilities were being overthrown. A new world view was being formed. This stuff was beyond human comprehension. A spiritual trans- formation and renovation of mind was taking place. The world was turned upside down. A new reality was forming, eclipsing the old. His human cognition and biases were tilting upward. The supernatural was invading the natural.

Most remarkable were the teachings, even sur- passing the miracles. No one had ever talked like this before.

"...how can one enter into a strong man's house, and spoil his goods, except he first bind the strong man?"

(Matt. 12:29)

What did he mean? How was this to be understood? There was meat to his words and sayings.

The most shocking social implications concerning Jesus of Nazareth was his inherent disdain for the religious authorities. He was actually taking on the most learned and respected men of the day. Hundreds of years of tradition and deeply entrenched institutions were being assailed. This was a war. Who was this man? Everything he said or did was a marvel.

This Jesus was boldly, fearlessly, combatively backing down the most revered men of his day. Face to face with the ensuing conflicts, he was excoriating the priests of the Sanhedrin and obliterating their arguments. All they could do was go silent. Every incident was a complete embarrassment, a humiliation. The confrontations were extraordinary. The supernatural world was violently colliding with the temporal. It was spiritual war personified.

All Israel, the entire Jewish world, esteemed the learned Sanhedrin and held them in the highest respect. They were regarded with reverential fear. This man opposed them all, and he wasn't short of attitude or words. He was staid, steeled, and prepared for conflict whenever they challenged.

It didn't take long for the first encounter to take place. The news spread fast about all that was happening in Galilee, and it eventually reached Jerusalem.

When the Sanhedrin heard what he was saying and doing in the upper regions, several envoys of the high court were sent out to confront him.

They must have been particularly bothered to make such a long journey. It was an eighty-mile trek from the fabled city of Jerusalem to the humble fishing villages that surrounded the Sea of Galilee. In fact, it was at least a four to five days' journey on foot.

The Jewish priests were far beyond annoyed under- taking such a journey. They were clearly bothered. They had to confront and rectify the situation before it got out of hand. For them to walk those many miles to deal with the Jesus problem spoke volumes about their anxious concerns.

When the Sanhedrin first confronted Jesus, it didn't take long for the sparks to fly.

"Why do thy disciples transgress the tradition
of the elders? for they wash not their hands
when they eat bread.

But he answered and said unto them, why
do ye also transgress the commandment of
God by your tradition?"

(Matt. 2–3)

And so it began. His answer ignited the conflict. From
that point it would escalate, continuing unto the inevitable
conclusion—his violent death.

The antagonist enters the story, for with this incident,
entered the Pharisees of the Sanhedrin—the minions of the great
adversary. It is no different today than it was two thousand years
ago.

Whoever despises religion is not alone. So did Jesus. He
pressed the conflict, further insulting them to their faces. He
called them hypocrites. He had no patience nor shortage of
words for the self-righteous priests who considered themselves
above it all and in the know.

They thought of themselves a cut above the common
people. These were the so-called *learned priests*. They were the
intellectuals of the day. Jesus with the sword of his mouth cut
them to pieces.

"Ye serpents, ye generation of vipers, how can
ye escape the damnation of hell?"

(Matt. 23:33)

He let it fly. There was no shortage of words. His followers
were shocked to the core. What in the world was he doing? Yet

his disciples were, themselves, still laboring under the spell of the learned elders. They began correcting and rebuking him for insulting the revered men who had come all the way from Jerusalem.

They didn't comprehend; they couldn't grasp it, for they were still mentally under their control. The Sanhedrin to them were another kind of pharaoh.

"Then came his disciples, and said unto him, Knowest thou that the Pharisees were offended, after they heard this saying?

"But he answered and said, every plant, which my heavenly Father hath not planted, shall be rooted up.

Let them alone: they are blind leaders of the blind. And if the blind lead the blind, both shall fall into the ditch"

(Matt. 15:14)

Take heed. The caution and warning to them was difficult to accept, and so it is. There were years— indeed centuries—of tradition to consider. Such is the case to this day.

Christ's warning is for all in every age: Let them alone. The world had fallen into the ditch of religious traditionalism, ignorantly following the so-called learned elders and their doctrines. Solomon said it best.

"The thing that hath been, it is that which shall be; and that which is done is that which shall be done: and there is no new thing under the sun"

(Eccl. 1:9)

The man from Galilee struck the match. He lit the fuse. It was burning, and burning quickly.

"Ye serpents, ye generation of vipers..."

How did he get away with these insults? Where was this going?

The whole Jewish nation followed after the learned Sanhedrin elders. This guy Jesus stood in open defiance, totally opposing their authority. The diatribes he launched were like weapons of war. He seemed to relish and welcome the altercations.

Tradition is the enemy of Truth.

But tucked into this amazing and remarkable episode was also a hidden prophecy? Was it irony, a coincidence, or a significant detail that was overlooked?

Here was a statement that was more than a statement—it was a prophecy.

"Every plant, which my heavenly Father hath not planted, shall be rooted up"

(Matt. 15:13)

This was not merely a clever turn of phrase or casual hyperbole, but something that would manifest down the road. It was of tremendous prophetic significance. It was something that would literally take place, but more importantly have a tremendous spiritual impact for those who would have eyes to see and ears to hear.

Nathanael and the others could not sort out the meaning of these unprecedented confrontations. They were all shocked to their core as they observed the Jewish priests tongue-tied and unable to deal with his superior logic. They could not respond. They could only stare with a blank face.

This Jesus had superior knowledge and authority. It struck the adversaries dumb. It was obvious the priests could not deal with him. The disciples were dismayed. Who was this Jesus of Nazareth?

Nathanael must have feared there could be repercussions down the road. In fact, as a follower, he might even become implicated. It was a dangerous proposition to follow this man, but Nathanael was mesmerized. He was captivated. He had to follow. How could he turn back at this point; it was unthinkable. It was so compelling that for Nathanael, the risks far outweighed the danger.

What had been promised—that he would see greater things—was happening. They were coming to pass. He was seeing them with his own eyes. It was exhilarating, but at the same time disquieting. Yet the promise of angels ascending and descending had left the forefront of his thinking.

But like a good screenplay, slipped in into the story, was a little detail. A detail that has, understandably, been overlooked.

Often times a clue may be introduced early into a story. Unless one saw the movie or read the book numerous times, it would go unnoticed. It is quietly placed into the narrative and almost imperceptible, but nonetheless it is key. Such was the case in the story of Nathanael.

In fact, the clue is a key that unlocks a door that has long been shut to the world. It would be the opening of the locked door which would allow Nathanael to advance to the ultimate transcendental promise of seeing angels ascending and descending on the Son of Man.

It is the key intended for everyone. It is for all, but there is as caveat. While it is *intended* for all, it is only for those who are willing to use it.

This key was impossible, though, for the religious and learned people of that day. They were too invested.

The key is subtle, which is why most all have stumbled over it. For those, today, who would seek to discover the key, the problem has become even passed. There are massive complications.

After thousands of years, it has been deeply buried. It has been covered by myths, legends, false histories and religious traditions. There are also the Sanhedrin who guard them. The Sanhedrin have always con- trolled the people—and control them still.

In order to overcome their control, there must come a personal intellectual honesty to confront former assumptions. A new brave confrontation with what has, heretofore, been taken for granted and blindly accepted as truth.

It is today's personal confrontation with the Sanhedrin.

The religious presumptions of the past must be recognized and dealt with in order to recognize and discover the key. It will take stomach and internal fortitude.

But the discovery cannot be seen with the eyes or heard with the ear. It is not perceptible with everyday human senses, yet it must be perceived, nonetheless. It must be uncovered and re-discovered.

The Sanhedrin took a position of knowing. They were puffed up with knowledge and unable to receive the truth. Their minds were full. There was no room for the truth.

As it was then, so it is today. The dogmas, the doc- trines, the myths and religious biases have filled the mind, but they are passé. It is time to empty the cache and make room for the truth. It is time to empty the influence of the Sanhedrin.

Chapter 3

THE FIG TREE

ဪ

After three years of intensive and exhausting effort, mile upon mile of walking, endless teaching episodes throughout the land, no set place to eat or sleep, Jesus with his twelve disciples entered the final leg of their journey. They were heading on to Jerusalem. The disciples were yet unaware that it was to be the final week of his life.

As they traveled along the way, Jesus began to prepare the men for what lay ahead. Upon approaching the old city of Jericho, some nineteen miles east of Jerusalem, he told them the parable of the fig tree. The parable was a story about a lack of righteousness in the land, and he used the fig tree in the parable to illustrate his point.

After three years of taxing work there was relatively little change in the general thinking and behavior of the people. The fig tree in the story was a reference to Israel. A nation that was incapable of producing the fruit of righteousness.

Christ had taught, fed, and healed people, but the effect of the three years' work had not produced the kind of fruit he was looking for. What was he expecting to see in the land? He was looking for a nation that would bear the fruit of righteousness. But after three years of his ministry, the people were essentially unchanged.

Thirteen centuries had come and gone from the time of Moses when the Ten Commandments had been given, but the old covenant had not produced any measurable results. There was no fruit, virtually no change in the people.

It wasn't because of a failure of his ministry though. It was because of the pervasive nature of the religious system that grew out of the law. The prevailing religious grip was so strong and so deeply rooted in the people that the fruit of righteousness was choked out. It was overwhelmed by the weeds of the failed old covenant.

A list of the specific sins is not necessary. Suffice it to say, the Hebrew people were still defrauding one another and, in multiple ways, behaving unseemly. They were violating and transgressing every single law of the Ten Commandments.

From the highest office of the priesthood down to the common man, there were none who were righteous. The list of transgressions against the law of the Jews was endless and manifestly obvious.

The general impact of the religion, in terms of producing righteousness in the nation, was of no effect. It was not happening. It was powerless to produce the fruit of righteousness. It didn't matter what station of life one was in. The fig tree in the parable represented a tree without the fruit of righteousness. This was the Hebrew people.

As the group proceeded toward Jerusalem, Jesus was relating to them this general state of affairs through the story. Israel, as he saw it, Israel was a fig tree barren of fruit. It was a story in which the fig tree would become manifestly obvious in a short period of time.

> "A certain man had a fig tree planted in his vineyard; and he came and sought fruit thereon, and found none. Then said he unto the dresser of his vineyard, Behold, these three years I come seeking fruit on this fig tree, and find none: cut it down; why cumbereth it the ground? And he answering said unto him, Lord, let it alone this year also, till I shall dig about it, and dung it: And if it bears fruit, well: and if not, then after that thou shalt cut it down."
>
> **(Luke 13:6–9)**

What is fascinating about the parable is that it was also a prophecy. Israel, the Hebrews, could not produce the fruit of righteousness though rooted firmly in the law. When the Jews did not recognize their visitation (Emmanuel-God with us) it was as though the fertilizer represented in the parable was ineffective. The prophecy in the story would come to pass forty years later, after Christ's appearance on earth. Israel, the fig tree, was cut down.

Just as was foretold in the parable, in 70 AD the Romans were the sharp instrument of destruction that would cut down the fig tree. The Roman soldiers liter- ally destroyed the place. They cut down every tree and killed millions of Jews. They destroyed the temple, eliminating all the sacrifices and at least a million more Jews were sold into slavery.

Then, sixty years later, at the Bar Kokhba revolt, the Roman emperor Hadrian had the name of the city Jerusalem changed to Aelia Capitolina and the name of Israel changed to Palestine. Everything was obliterated.

The fig tree in the parable was cut down, and it was all about the Hebrews, the law, their temple, and the land of Israel. It was all cut down. The prophecy in the parable was fulfilled— And *if it bear fruit, well: and if not, then after that thou shalt cut it down.*

The disciples listened intently, but at the particular moment, the full understanding was not clear to them, but to Nathanael, in particular, it may have struck a more meaningful note.

It may have reminded him of the first incident where Jesus saw him standing under a fig tree. Most certainly, though, the magnitude of the fig tree with its prophetic overtones and its symbolic meaning would have to unfold in the ensuing days. At that moment, the full meaning of the parable to them would have to wait.

It is important to point out the appearance of the fig tree at the outset of Nathanael's calling. It was introduced in a subtle way. Few notice its introduction into the fabric of the story. In fact, hardly anyone notices it at all. It is just a small detail tucked into the story. Nathanael was simply standing under a fig tree. But it is introduced and noted in the New Testament specifically for an important reason. It wasn't just any tree. It was a fig tree. It was an important detail. The appearance and meaning of the fig tree would factor significantly, and grow exponentially not only for Nathanael, but for all.

At the outset, hidden within the story, is the obscure small detail of the fig tree. As attention is drawn to the tree, it picks up momentum. The numerous times it appears bears significance. What is happening? How was this missed? What does it mean?

Introduced into the story, there is a growing aware- ness of this strange clue. It is a clue so skillfully and quietly woven, so carefully inserted into the general narrative that it slips by going unnoticed. The fig tree. Yet such a great clue that was present throughout the panorama of Jewish history. It was always there just not recognized.

The clue was not only present in Jewish history; Jesus also referred to the fig tree as a sign of the future. What he said would turn out to be prophetic.

"When his branch is yet tender, and putteth
forth leaves, ye know that summer is nigh"
(Matt. 24:32)

He spoke this prophecy during the last days of his earthly life in the famous Olivet discourse.

As a fig tree has a certain moment when its spring- time leaves signal a new seasons of summer coming, so also there would come signs that would indicate the nearness of the coming of the kingdom of God. Here again, he uses the fig tree to convey the meaning.

The land of Israel in the prophecy was characterized as a fig tree. And when a tree puts forth leaves it is the sign that summer is near, but the point is the *fig* tree is summoned to our attention again. There were countless varieties of trees in Israel, so why the fig tree?

While the introduction to the fig tree quietly commences with the Nathanael incident, it finds even more momentum with the prophetic parable. The fact of the matter is the nation of Israel had always been identified with the fig tree.

For example, there was the record of the fig tree at a notable moment in the life of Jeremiah the great Jewish prophet.

A trek backwards through Jewish history, to the sixth century BC, has Jeremiah called to do a most difficult task. But in one particular experience, the context of his prophetic calling was defined and explained in a vision. It concerned the fig tree's fruit.

So, once again a window in the spiritual skies opens relating to God's fixation with the fig tree.

Here is what was related concerning the fig tree and figs:

Jeremiah was not well liked by the religious authorities of his day either. Actually he was despised and hated! As it was with so many prophets of old, he was called to tell the nation of Israel some horrendous and unsettling news. It was information they did not want to hear.

While God is longsuffering, the time comes when he must bring judgment. After repeated warnings, if there is no turning from evil and amending of ways, God intervenes. Before a catastrophic judgment, he sends a final warning. He uses prophets as his proxies to convey his ultimatum.

It was an unenviable task for Jeremiah, and it was costly. The calling would cause him to suffer greatly at the hands of the religious authorities and also at the hand of Israel's reigning king.

Now look at the transcendental supernatural vision as recorded in the twenty-fourth chapter of the book of Jeremiah and what he was told to do.

> "The Lord shewed me, and, behold, two baskets of figs were set before the temple of the Lord...
> One basket had very good figs, even like the figs that are first ripe: and the other basket had very bad figs, which could not be eaten, they were so bad.
> Then said the Lord unto me, What seest thou, Jeremiah? And I said, Figs; the good figs, very good; and the evil, very evil, that cannot be eaten, they are so evil."
>
> **(Jer. 24:1–3)**

Figs again! Here is found, once again, the mention of figs, this time within the context and in the panorama of Jewish history. Why the figs? What is the leading to? What is up with figs and fig trees?

Perhaps Jesus may have been recounting this story in the life of Jeremiah to his followers as they made their way to Jerusalem. Who knows? It most certainly could have been in his mind because he knew what was coming again for the temple and for the city of Jerusalem.

Whether it was or not, the episode in the time of Jeremiah was written down to instruct the world about the reason for the destruction of the first temple and the carrying away of the Hebrew people to Babylon, Jeremiah talked about it in the context of figs.

So let's recap. We have the fig tree under which Nathanael stood. We have the parable of the fig tree. We have the prediction of the fig tree, and now we have the comparison of the figs of the fig tree. The figs were both good and evil. The massive point is the preponderance of fig trees and figs that become apparent.

Although Jeremiah's mention of good and evil figs comes as a parable, it calls to mind and invokes a certain recollection. It is the term good and evil. This term is recounted in the book of Genesis where the fig tree is first noted.

The clue that is so clearly inserted throughout the entire Bible is of course the fig tree, but its first mention is referenced at the beginning in the book of Genesis.

Adam and Eve partook of the fruit of the Tree of Knowledge of Good and Evil. As a result, they found themselves naked and hence covered themselves with fig leaves.

The fig tree became a symbol of the Tree of Knowledge of Good and Evil, but the meaning of the clue has an important connection with the Jewish high court, the Sanhedrin.

That connection is up the road nineteen miles from the moon god city of Jericho at the village of Bethphage.

Chapter 4

APPROACHING JERUSALEM

৬৹৵৶

The entourage did not stop in Jericho; they just passed through. The son of David was hard pressed to make it to Jerusalem before the Passover celebration, which was to happen in a few days.

He may have recalled the history of the ancient city of Jericho though. The city had undergone significant changes since then as Herod the Great had rebuilt it. Jericho had been destroyed when the Hebrews entered the land some thirteen hundred years prior, but Herod had since constructed palaces and ornate buildings in the city.

He used Jericho as an escape from the cold of Jerusalem during the winter months. But as they passed through the city, the memory of the history of Jericho may have crossed the mind of Jesus.

Jericho had been known as the moon-god city. The moon-god was synonymous with the lesser light in the heavens, or the female deity.

There were many female goddesses worshiped in those days, and sadly those deities also had been embraced by the Jews. They even brought reverence of the female deity into the temple of God. Moon-god worship was prevalent throughout the fertile crescent and to an extent it bled into the religious life of the Hebrews. It was for that reason God had visited Jerusalem and the first temple with destruction six centuries prior. Jesus was well aware of a coming second destruction in the not too distant future.

Today, of course, the moon-god is embraced by the Muslim world as Allah. This is clearly evident in that over every mosque in the world is the crescent moon. The crescent moon is also on the flags of every Muslim nation.

God's commentary and his thoughts concerning the moon-god Islam was apparent and conclusive when he crushed Jericho, the moon-god city, under the leader-ship of Joshua during earlier centuries.

In the end, at the final outcome at the end of the age, just as the women in Revelation twelve stands on the moon, so will Israel stand in victory over the malignant moon-god.

But Israel, in the first century, was sliding backward toward the universal world belief with the moon-god, and both the temple and the priesthood had become corrupted and compromised. It was only a matter of time before history would repeat and the city of Jerusalem along with the temple would be destroyed again.

Had Jesus called to mind those far off days, it would have served to underscore the present reason for his mission.

In any event he was hard pressed to reach Jerusalem. The decadence of the priesthood, as in centuries past, had ripened, and once again filled to the brim of indignation. The sins of the priesthood had reached heaven and were now overflowing God's cup.

But even though the people had all known of the previous catastrophic destruction, they had not learned. History was knocking at the door, but no one was hearing let alone answering.

Jesus was not only coming to warn them about a second destructive judgment by the "prince of Rome" (the destruction of the city and temple), he was bringing in an astonishing change.

His mind was not focused on Herod's new Jericho. He was just passing through pressing on to the big city.

It was nineteen miles to Jerusalem from Jericho on a road that was well traveled. The road was the primary artery, an entry into the city of Jerusalem from the east. The main road was traveled upon several times a year, but this time devout Jews would be making their way to Jerusalem for the Passover feast. The feast was to take place in a few short days.

Many of those early arrivals on the road may have walked in close proximity to Jesus, not realizing who it was. There was no way to apprehend the momentous events which were about to take place. But before they would enter the city, they would pass by the village of Bethphage.

As they walked along, they would have been talking, or at least thinking about, the great Passover festival they were headed for and what it meant. They would have been remembering the great and historic occasion.

The Hebrews were required by Jewish law to make three pilgrimages to Jerusalem a year. They were to keep the three great feasts tied to Jewish history, but the Passover feast was special and the most important. It was elevated above all the other feasts.

It was in their history, while held in bondage in the land of Egypt, that God supernaturally intervened. It was then that he provided a way out (The Exodus) from their four-hundred-year enslavement, (actually four hundred and thirty years) and the memory of the event was to be kept in perpetuity.

The Egyptians were punished with ten plagues as they relentlessly tried to hold onto their captive Jewish slaves.

The last of the ten plagues was the straw that broke the camel's back. In it was the plague that convinced the pharaoh to let God's people go.[4]

God would kill the firstborn of every household. The only means for preventing the plague was to take the blood of a lamb and paint it on the lintel and the door posts.

Every house that had the blood of the lamb would be exempt and not be visited with death to the first- born. The last plague came upon all the houses where there was no blood displayed on the door. The failure to do so was a death warrant.

The house of pharaoh was visited with death as his son died that very night. Inevitably, Pharaoh relented, and let the Hebrew people go. This was the Passover feast which commemorated those days.

As the people joyously walked the nineteen-mile road to Jerusalem they could not have calculated the irony. How sacred the moment, walking in such close proximity to Jesus the Lamb of God, who in just a few short days by the shedding of his own blood would become the fulfillment of the Passover.

Remarkably there was more to the crucifixion of Christ by the shedding of his blood and the fulfillment of the Passover that was accomplished at his death.

Beyond the discussion of the coming Passover along the well-traveled road, there was another topic of conversation. They had to have been discussing the most recent miraculous healing to a blind man named Bartimaeus. But they had seen many healings and miracles during the past three years. This was nothing new. What was surprising was something else.

"And it came to pass, that as he was come nigh
unto Jericho, a certain blind man sat by the
way side begging:
And hearing the multitude pass by, he
asked what it meant.
And they told him, that Jesus of Nazareth
passeth by.
And he cried, saying, Jesus, thou son of
David, have mercy on me"
(Luke 18:35–39)

Jesus called him out and totally healed him of blindness.

No doubt this miraculous incident was in the fore- front of their minds on their way to Jerusalem because Bartimaeus continued to follow after them as they journeyed on to the great city. He was right there with them. His presence was a reminder of the miracle of healing.

But the fact that Bartimaeus called him *son of David* is what stuck in their minds and excited them because they knew all the prophecies.

"And there shall come forth a rod out of the
stem of Jesse [father of King David], and a
Branch shall grow out of his roots:

And the spirit of the Lord shall rest upon
him, the spirit of wisdom and understanding,
the spirit of counsel and might, the spirit of
knowledge and of the fear of the Lord;

And shall make him of quick understanding
in the fear of the Lord: and he shall not judge
after the sight of his eyes, neither reprove after
the hearing of his ears:

But with righteousness shall he judge the
poor, and reprove with equity for the meek of
the earth: and he shall smite the earth: with the
rod of his mouth, and with the breath of his
lips shall he slay the wicked"

(Isa 11:1-4)

The disciples knew all the prophecies, but perhaps the
prophetic words of Jeremiah were the most poignant.

"Behold, the days come, saith the Lord, that
I will raise unto David a righteous Branch,
and a King shall reign and prosper, and shall
execute judgment and justice in the earth.

In his days Judah shall be saved, and Israel
shall dwell safely..."

(Jeremiah 23:5–6)

And so hearing Jesus being called the son of David struck
a chord. The healing of Bartimaeus as he continued on with them
was living proof that this was the promised son of David. This
was their great hope, and now they brimmed with excitement.

As they approached Jerusalem, their anticipation mounted with each step.

Here was the very son of David walking with them along the road to Jerusalem; here was the son of David to deliver all Israel out of the grip of the Roman Empire and re-establish, once again, David's kingdom. The prophecy of Jeremiah was being fulfilled right before them as they walked toward the city. Finally, the coming king had come. This for certain was in their minds as it was underscored by the healing of Bartimaeus.

Shortly, all of Jerusalem would be engulfed in the fire of their enthusiasm. The fervor of the disciples would ignite the city. The disciples were primed to spread the news.

The healing of Bartimaeus was a powerful catalyst that played into the setup for the great trap.

The exciting stage was set for Christ's triumphal entry into Jerusalem, but the reality of the setup was beyond the grasp of the disciples.

It was a trap that they themselves were inadvertently baiting. However, on the Jerusalem ahead of them, lay the village of Bethphage. And what would happen there would have great significance indeed, though none at the time recognized it.

Chapter 5

THE SECRET OF BETHPHAGE

Thanks to the phenomenal research of Dr. Ernest Martin, we now have powerful insight into the historic place, Bethphage.[5]

As they approached the city of Jerusalem, two of his disciples were summoned to go ahead into the village of Bethphage. There, it was told them, they would find a colt or donkey upon which the coming king would ride triumphant into Jerusalem.

Bethphage was more than just the location for the animal transport which would carry Christ into the fabled city. Bethphage was an important religious place. Many of the coming events of the last week of Jesus' life would involve the village of Bethphage.

Bethphage was strategically located a little beyond two thousand cubits [about twelve hundred yards] from the Jewish temple. It was situated on the north- ern half of the Mount of Olives on the east side of the mount.

The Mount of Olives has both northern and south- ern mounds. In between the two halves is a lower elevation of several hundred yards, and through this pass ran a nineteen-mile roadway. The roadway that ran between the two halves of the Mount of Olives was the last stretch of the nineteen-mile road that began at Jericho. The roadway led all the way to the temple of the Jews. It was this last portion of the nineteen- mile road that Jesus, riding the donkey, would take to the temple.

When the Jewish pilgrims would come to keep the various Sabbaths and feasts, they would pass by the village of Bethphage slightly north of the well-traveled road. The road was also nearby the altar of the red heifer, which like Bethphage, was situated just outside the camp of Israel.

Adjacent to Bethphage was the village of Bethany where Mary Martha and Lazarus lived. It was the same Lazarus that Jesus raised from the dead and his traditional tomb site is there in Bethany. Whether or not this is the real tomb no one knows for certain—but since tradition is almost always wrong, probably not.

Bethany was where he would stay with his friends the night after his historic and memorable ride into the city.

Bethphage had an important meaning that sheds great light on the meaning of the fig tree. It is a the present.

The Jewish high religious court was called the Sanhedrin. The highly regarded elders of the Jewish court had special locations where they gathered both inside and outside the camp for making important determinations, decisions, and judgments.

Inside the camp they would meet within the temple precinct at the place called the House of Hewn Stones. It was just a few meters to the south of the altar of burnt offerings. The altar of burnt offering stood in front and just a few meters east of the door into the inner temple.

It was inside the temple environs where the high court would eventually make the official determination as to whether Jesus was guilty or not. And inside the temple area was where they convened at the House of Hewn Stones.

But the Sanhedrin had an additional location for making determinations and judgments, and that location was at Bethphage. The quiet village that came to be called Bethphage was selected as the location for daily legal and important matters that occurred outside the camp.

Since there were various issues; such as problems of sin, sicknesses, and social issues of divorce, com- plaints, lawsuits. There had to be a location outside the camp to deal with these problems. It was the priests of the Sanhedrin that would preside over these numerous and sundry matters at Bethphage.

In addition, Bethphage was the location where they would meet to decide issues that pertained to such things as census or polling.

Polling or census-taking had to take place outside the camp in order to guard against sickness. If a person were sick they would pollute the camp and make it unclean. So polls and censuses had to take place outside the camp. This was also true for taxation. Outside the camp was where the poll tax was collected.

Again, if a sick person were coming to pay tax, it had to be done outside the camp for the same important reason. They had to collect everyone's tax money. Again, so the camp would not be polluted and made unclean—for everyone had to pay taxes clean or unclean—this had to be done outside the camp.

These priests were also responsible for ceremonially dealing with the sick. This was according to Jewish law. The altar of the red heifer nearby, which had the burnt ashes of the animal, was for cleansing the sick. The ashes of the red heifer were applied by the priests. This was all done outside the camp.

These men also dealt with people that needed cleansing from handling dead bodies. A person handling a dead body had to be ceremonially cleansed with the ashes of the red heifer and they were not allowed to enter the camp for seven days. It all had to be done outside the camp.

The priests in Bethphage also had to make determinations on crimes committed outside the environs of the camp, such as those pertaining to thieves and murderers and the like.

But what is most interesting and compelling about Bethphage is the meaning of the name. It had a hidden meaning.

Bethphage meant the House of Unripe Figs.[6] The idea of the meaning of the name is a throwback to the time of Adam and Eve, and it gives insight into Jewish understanding of sin.

As the story goes, Adam and Eve ate from the Tree of Knowledge of Good and Evil. As a result of their transgression, they found themselves to be naked. What did they do? They covered themselves with fig leaves. The leaves that came from the Tree of the Forbidden Fruit. Hence the fig tree to the Jews was synonymous with the Tree of Knowledge of Good and Evil.

The idea for the venue of Bethphage—the place outside the camp where the Sanhedrin met—was associated with figs, and now unripe figs had tremendous significance.

Sin was defined by the Ten Commandments—their law. How can good and evil be understood without the law? The law defines good and evil and thus it too was associated with the fig tree.

The priests of the Sanhedrin had to have a clean image. They had to maintain the respect that they were not tainted or influenced by sin. So the place of meeting outside the camp for this reason was called the House of Unripe Figs. Not only was the name Bethphage evocative, they actually believed they were beyond the reproach of sin.

The idea of the name was that, even though they had a venue outside the camp, they were not tainted by the influence of sin. Their person and their judgments were held in the highest and utmost regard. Unlike the general population, they were untainted and free of sin. And this was the reason for the name Bethphage.

Figs had a definite and clear meaning to Jews. Figs were associated with the fig leaves and how Adam and Eve covered their nakedness. They took those leaves from the very tree from which they had eaten—the Tree of Knowledge of Good and Evil.

It is also gives better understanding and points to the meaning of Jeremiah's vision of the good figs and the evil figs.

The Tree of Knowledge of Good and Evil was the fig tree, and the fig tree was associated with the law.

The House of Unripe Figs, Bethphage, carried with it the intimation that the learned and high Sanhedrin priests were not tainted by ripened figs, or sin. Sin represented by figs in the name of Bethphage had not ripened and therefore had no influence affecting the priestly judgments. Bethphage, the House of Unripe Figs, and the priests were beyond reproach. These men were experts in the law and, therefore, beyond its condemnation.

The suggestion of unripe figs conveyed the meaning that sin had no effect on them because they were unripe. Therefore, they could judge righteously—or so they thought.

Bethphage is tremendously important in under- standing how the Jews felt about sin, the meaning of the Tree of Knowledge of Good and Evil, the fig tree, and the law of the Jews.

At the beginning, Jesus saw Nathanael standing under the fig tree or under what it represented, i.e. the law. And so throughout scripture and the history of Israel the nation, there is an association with the fig tree.

The fig tree is everywhere: Nathanael is seen under the fig tree; there is the parable of the fig tree, the prophetic forecast of the fig tree, Jeremiah and the good figs and bad figs, Bethphage house of unripened figs, and then Adam and Eve and the fig leaves with which they feebly tried to cover themselves.

"For every tree is known by his own fruit.
For of thorns men do not gather figs, nor of a
bramble bush gather they grapes"

(Luke 6:44)

In the case of Israel and the Jews and their law there was none—no righteous fruit. The law of the Jews, i.e. the Ten Commandments, could not produce righteousness. It was a dead covenant.

So Bethphage, the House of Unripe Figs, was set up outside the camp for the priests of the Sanhedrin to judge the people, and according to the very name of the village, it represented justice.

Israel was given the law by Moses, so Israel itself was also symbolized and represented by the fig tree.

The notion that the priests' judgments could be free from the effect of sin was an idealistic presumption.

There has never been a mortal who has come into this world that has escaped the horrific nature and effect of sin. It is evident to this day. Everyone will die because of breaking the Law. This is the effect of sin. The whole issue of this life is about sin and its terrible and debilitating power over the human body and mind. There is simply no way a man or woman is exempt and free from the predicament.

The men who considered themselves experts in the law were, in a sense, doing the same as Adam and Eve. As Adam and Eve tried to cover themselves with fig leaves, so did the high priest try to cover themselves with law. Just like Adam and Eve it was all in vain.

The high-minded Sanhedrin did not believe that they had the same problem as the masses. In their conceit, they carried themselves as though they were a cut above. The priests' superior air brought them into conflict with Jesus. From the very beginning, he was at odds with the ruling religious elite. Their puffed up and inflated minds, clothed by the fig leaves of the law, were about to make the greatest blunder in the history of jurisprudence.

They were about to kill their own king. So much for the House of Unripe Figs.

Chapter 6

PALM SUNDAY: THE TRAP

ᔾᔤ

Palm Sunday, or the day Christ rode triumphant into Jerusalem[7] (history is not clear on exactly which day of the week it was) marked the beginning of the end. It was the hair-trigger event that would change the world, but the true extent of the event remarkably is lost in tradition. To the multitudes, it is the arrival of Easter week. It happens every year, no big deal— except that it was a big *big* deal.

At first glance, the idea of Palm Sunday seems like a kind of passive holiday. It is to so many just a traditional religious observance. A time for the Easter bunny, cute little chicks and of course Easter egg hunts. For the religious, it means the introduction to Christ passion week, but that's about it. It is a historical remembrance at best. But its real significance is buried deep beneath religious ceremony. The secret of Palm Sunday is hidden from view. In reality, it was a gigantic snare. A trap.

In film writing parlance—if this were a movie script—it would be characterized as the inciting incident. The inciting incident is the event in a movie which ignites and catapults forward the rest of the film.

The triumphal entry of Jesus into the city of Jerusalem was the master stroke of the wisdom of God. It was a carefully organized plan that was written before the foundation of the world. It was the inciting incident.

Insight into the plan—which was pre-determined— was made known to Jesus. He knew of the inciting incident and what was truly intended with regard to his triumphal entry. It was not what the people commonly assume.

"Then answered Jesus and said unto them,
Verily, verily, I say unto you, The Son can
do nothing of himself, but what he seeth the
Father do: for what things so ever he doeth,
these also doeth the Son likewise" (John 5:19).

There are other references which suggest that Jesus was privy to the plan. He was alerted and had a heads up as to what was about to really take place. All the scriptures indicate he knew the wisdom and rational behind the plan. He knew the script.

When the entourage arrived in Jerusalem, the disciples brought with them the great swelling idea that Jesus, the great prophet great miracle worker, had come to set up and restore the long awaited kingdom of David. Remember, it was the healing of Bartimaeus that sparked their emotional frenzy. This Jesus was the very son of David coming to restore the kingdom of David. The disciples had spread the news through- out the city, and it caused a massive turnout.

This was not a hard idea to sell to the Jewish people, especially those in Jerusalem, because not far from their temple, watching and standing over the city was the Antonia fortress of their Roman captors. The ever- present Romans and with their fortress was a galling reminder to the Jews of their subservience to Rome. Each and every day the hope for a restored kingdom of David was present in their minds. Now their very hope was riding into town on a donkey. Thousands attended the entry shouting "Hosanna to the King." It was unbelievable.

But his entry into the city was more than what met the eye of the revelers. It was deeper than what could be seen by superficial observation. It was a much bigger plan. It was a setup. It was a trap. The intent of the orchestrated spectacle was designed to enrage the Sanhedrin.

While Christ had foretold of his own death, the disciples did not understand; they just didn't get it. On the contrary, they thought the word of the prophets Jeremiah and Isaiah was coming to pass right before their eyes.

> "In those days, and at that time, will I cause the Branch of righteousness to grow up unto David; and he shall execute judgment and righteous- ness in the land"
>
> **(Jeremiah 33:15)**

> "And there shall come forth a rod out of the stem of Jesse [father of King David], and a Branch shall grow out of his roots"
>
> **(Isa. 11:1)**

There were other prophecies concerning the restored Davidic kingdom that attended their thinking, but there was no way they could apprehend and see the big picture.

When he rode in, they believed with all their hearts that David's kingdom was about to be restored—that the time of prophecy was at hand.

This notion was what the disciples thought, and they brought the excitement of it into Jerusalem. As a result, the idea swept over and engulfing all the people of Jerusalem; the whole city was on fire. They bought it. It was a masterful sales job.

God had a very different plan, however.

Nevertheless, this naive hope spread throughout all Jerusalem, and it overwhelmed the city like a tsunami. No one saw the triumphal entry Palm Sunday as a trap set for the Sanhedrin.

Hope suggested that this was the prophet Jesus from Galilee who commanded mighty signs and who had come to set up David's kingdom. Surely this was the rod from the stem of Jesse; this was he whom Isaiah foretold.

Certainly this was the consuming thought and was on the lips of all the people. The disciples had lit a fire, and the city was consumed with the passion of the hope that the kingdom of David was about to be restored. The long wait was over. *Hosanna to the king!*

But unbeknown to the people, the very entry and the praises of hosanna was intended as a snare. It was a trap set for the Sanhedrin, and baited by arousing the people of the city. The masses inadvertent had baited the hook, and the religious authorities' bit. And they bit hard.

While the triumphal entry of Jesus was, nevertheless, a proclamation of a kingdom, it was to be an inner kingdom, and not the one they had envisioned. But foremost, it was a proclamation purposefully intended to incite both the religious and civic authorities of the day.

The religious authorities could never have imagined that the triumphal entry was the trigger mechanism for the setting up of the real kingdom by inducing and fueling the fire of their hatred—a hatred which, in turn, precipitated their actions and led to the murder of Jesus Christ. How could they possibly have under- stood the wisdom of God?

> "But we speak the wisdom of God in a mystery,
> even the hidden wisdom, which God ordained
> before the world unto our glory:
> Which none of the princes of this world
> knew: for had they known it, they would not
> have crucified the Lord of glory"
>
> **(1 Cor 2:7–8)**

While the people shouted hosanna (praise the Lord) little did they themselves know they were actually baiting the hook. Their gaze was on the hope of a restored external kingdom of David: a kingdom in the physical external world, an immediate physical kingdom. Their idea of God's kingdom was totally misconstrued. And in addition, they had no concept that his kingdom could possibly include gentiles either.

This was what the they could not fathom.

The shouting continued as they gathered along the road. The people covered the last stretch of the nine- teen-mile road to the city with their coats and palm branches. Each palm branch and hosanna was a thorn in the side of the religious authorities.

The intensified tension in the air was unbearable to the priests, but to the people, it was just the opposite. It was sweet incense, a perfume. It was exhilarating. It was intoxicating.

The intensity of the moment would kick start the final moments of God's ingenious plan. It was the inciting incident. It would act as an accelerate amplifying the fears and hatreds of the self-righteous Sanhedrin. The authority of the Sanhedrin over the people was being shaken. The ax was being laid to the roots. Oil had been thrown on the fire.

The whole idea of praise to a man was repugnant to the Jewish Sanhedrin. It infuriated the priests who exalted in their law. And since they were the experts in the law, they saw the adoration and praise as a threat to their own power and authority. They cautioned Jesus and demanded he quiet the crowd.

> "And some of the Pharisees from among the multitude said unto him, Master, rebuke thy disciples.
>
> And he answered and said unto them, I tell you that, if these should hold their peace, the stones would immediately cry out"
>
> **(Luke 19:39–40)**

The priests, self-elevated in their own minds, had to find a way to stop what was at hand. It was time to act, and the situation called for something radical. This man had to be stopped.

And while the multitudes of admirers did not understand the real nature and depth of the triumphal entry and its true purpose, their adulation would shortly fade. In only a few days, their happiness would fall into great despair and sad disappointment.

Then they would all turn on Jesus and mock him. In just a few days, their hope of David's kingdom being restored would die.

In fact, the triumphal entry was extraordinarily successful. It had set in motion the wheels of destiny and the purposed plan. It perfectly played into the hands and hatreds of the religious detractors as none could see the master plan was moving forward. And while it looked as though the Jewish priests were in control, the contrary was true. God was in absolute control.

He was using their elevated hatreds to advance the plan. They could not stand the praise. It drove them mad. What they had heard from afar had now come home to roost. Their greatest fear had matured and had come to their turf. It had igniting their long smoldering angst. As he rode in triumphant, their recalcitrance exploded.

Now they sought earnestly a reason to stop him— even to kill him. Their identity, their purpose, their *very reason of existence* was in jeopardy.

This Jesus of Nazareth was beyond just a dangerous a man. He was, to them, the embodiment of evil and a real threat to not only their power but a usurper of their long-standing institutions. The stakes couldn't have been higher.

The religious authorities had been shaken to the core by the momentous event. The Sanhedrin had a real problem on their hands. Now they must diligently search for a legal reason to get him. They had to capture him and deal with him legally. It had to be legitimate according to the law.

There was no turning back now. They had taken the bait and unknowingly fallen into the trap.

"But we speak the wisdom of God in a mystery,
the hidden wisdom, which God predestined

before the ages to our glory, the wisdom which
none of the rulers of this age understood, for
if they had, they had understood it they would
not have crucified the Lord of glory"

(1 Cor. 2:7-8)

The triumphal entry on Palm Sunday was a great deal more
than bunnies, little chickens and Easter bonnets, and religious
observances if you will. It was the wisdom of God on display,
but unseen and not understood by the rulers of this age.

It seemed as though the events taking place were beginning
to cause things to spin out of control. Yet the truth of the matter
was that the stage had been set for the real *triumph*.

Chapter 7

THE NEXT DAY:
ABOUT TO GET ROUGH

ฅ๛๏

On arriving at the environs of the temple, he crossed a walking bridge which extended over the brook Kidron. The brook was east of the temple and flowed through the Kidron Valley. The bridge led up to the eastern gate of the temple complex. The eastern gate opened to a great courtyard six hundred feet on each side.

When he entered the temple's outer court, it was buzzing with activity. Inside the walls of the square were numerous tables that were arranged for the selling of doves for sacrifice. The doves were for the poor who could not afford the more expensive animals for sacrifice.

There were also tables set for the money changers. The changing of money was necessary, for coinage differed from place to place. The purpose was to make available the paying of tribute into the temple coffers for those who wanted to pay homage to God. The tribute was also the religious leaders chief source of income.

It was not hard to see that those who were running the tables were enjoying a lucrative business. They were overcharging for the doves, and the moneychangers were skimming far too much money with each exchange. The profiteering angered Jesus, but he held back his anger. He took mental notes, observing for what he would do the following next day.

That evening he took the bridge back across the brook Kidron to the road still strewn with the palm branches from earlier in the day. He passed by Bethphage to the neighboring village of Bethany where he would spend the night at the house of Mary Martha and Lazarus. The Passover feast was only a few days away, and the city was filling up with pilgrims as they poured into Jerusalem.

The next day, Jesus left Bethany for the temple again. He passed through Bethphage and walked the same road upon which he rode his donkey the day before. As he walked he approached a large solitary fig tree standing alongside the road. The fig tree was outside the camp nearby the altar of the red heifer. It was in the same vicinity where taxes were collected and where the census were taken. All of these locations were east of the temple and outside the camp.

The altar of the red heifer was the third altar that was part of the temple altar system. While the altar of burnt offerings and the altar of incense stood the red heifer was some two thousand cubits [a little than half a mile] from the temple curtain, yet still part of the temple altar complex. There were three altars to the temple, but only the altar of the red heifer was outside the camp and nearby to the fig tree.

The meaning of what Jesus was about to do with the fig tree, for most, remains just an historic event. The full meaning has been lost or at least not fully understood by those familiar with the episode. Here, once again, coming back into the discussion is the fig tree. Let's pick up the action and watch carefully what happens here. Take a note.

As he approached the fig tree, he was looking for fruit on the tree. He was looking for figs, but there were none.

It is important to keep in mind what had happened the previous day. He had seen numerous abuses in the temple square by those selling sacrificial doves at a handsome profit and those moneychangers skimming a good margin from the changing of the coinage.

Remember, the Sanhedrin derived their income from the tribute and tithes which came from the moneychangers who provided the means for how people could make contributions. They weren't about to disrupt the system that provided their livelihood.

The fig tree portrayed not only the Tree of Knowledge of Good and Evil—hence the law—but it also represented the nation of Israel. Jesus was about to make a great and symbolic statement. At the same time, he was living out and dramatizing what he had taught earlier in the parable of the fig tree. When he saw the fig tree having no fruit he literally cursed the tree. His disciples noticed what he had just done.

"And seeing a fig tree afar off having leaves, he
came, if haply he might find anything thereon:
and when he came to it, he found nothing but
leaves; for the time of figs was not yet.

And Jesus answered and said unto it, no
man eat fruit of thee hereafter forever. And his
disciples heard it."

(Mark 11:13-14)

Jesus was not just cursing the tree, because there was
nothing to satisfy his physical human appetite; he was making
an enormous statement. What he was doing to the fig tree had
significant implications and consequences. The cursing of the
fig tree would serve as an illustration and hence would convey
metaphorically what he would accomplish at his death. In addition
to the forgiveness of sins, he was highlighting and illustrating
something else, and that something has been obscured.

Jesus made it clear that everything he said and everything
he did had great depth of meaning. In the case of the cursed
fig tree, the frozen moment etched in the stonework of history
would become lost. The great meaning would be covered over
by the mildew of time and replaced by religious traditionalism.
And yet while intended for all time, the great meaning of the
cursed fig tree would simply fade out of sight.

But even at the moment of the cursing, men simply could
not grasp the depth of the meaning of Jesus' actions. What he
accomplished was an historic momentous event. The power
of the visual as a symbol and metaphor contains meaning that
would transcend linear doctrine.

It is of far greater benefit to have a visual picture in our
chamber of imagination then to recall a one- dimensional linear
hand written doctrine. Thus the magnitude of the cursing of
the fig tree takes on a greater depth of meaning when it is fully
understood. As a visual it can easily be called to mind.

The fig tree, had a massive root system. Not only did the roots run deep they spread wide. Just as the enormous root system of the fig tree goes deep into the earth and spreads out, so did the Jewish law. It was deeply rooted, spreading wide into all facets of Jewish life. Jesus was using the fig tree as a metaphoric illustration of that fact.

The law and the religion of the Jews was so pervasive it affected everything, every facet of life, but it did not produce the fruit of righteousness. This was the message. For there to come a departure from the law and Jewish tradition would have been unthinkable. It was so deeply rooted that, even amongst religious Jews today, it has dominion. It was therefore likened unto a mountain, and mountains are not easily moved. However:

"That whosoever shall say unto this mountain, be thou removed, and be thou cast into the sea; and shall not doubt in his heart, but shall believe that those things which he saith shall come to pass; he shall have whatsoever he saith"

(Mark 11:23)

Mountains could be moved just as trees with great roots could be made to wither and die. In the case of this particular fig tree, it would provide not only a stark visual reminder of the spiritual reality Jesus hoped to illustrate but would also play a central role in the great act that what was about to unfold.

When Jesus arrived at the temple several minutes later, he was about to do something inside the temple that shook things up literally. It too, while an actual historical event, was intended as a metaphor.

He was about to accomplish, in the temple, what he purposed in his heart the day before when he made mental notes. Before he could begin to turn things upside down, he had to make a statement. Cursing the fig tree was the statement. Now it was time to begin the overthrow of the problem, literally.

It was time to illustrate his desire and intention to make the change. He set himself to visually make another statement about the purpose for the house of God. He began to fix the problem.

What was evident in the illicit activity in the temple area was it had to be overthrown. Everything was com- promised. He had come to overthrow it all. The tables were the unrighteous fruit of a corrupt system—a tree, after all, is known by its fruit.

The tables evidenced the profligate activity of merchandising inside the temple. Clearly the law of the Jews could not produce the fruit of righteousness. He overturned the tables just after he cursed the fig tree. Now that the fig tree and what it represented had been taken out of the way, this is what was to be expected.

The fig tree which represented the law had to be uprooted. And for this to happen would be monumental. This was the reason why in the text the uprooting of the system was likened to a mountain. Hard to move a mountain.

He underscored the point by the symbolic throwing over the tables in the temple.

> "And he went into the temple, and began to cast out them that sold therein, and them that bought; Saying unto them, it is written, my house is the house of prayer: but ye have made it a den of thieves"

(Luke 19:45–46)

Today, people are the temple of God, but when tables are set for other purposes—when the priorities in the heart are aligned elsewhere—there comes a diminished prayer life, or none at all. God does nothing eternal without a voice on earth. His word must be spoken on earth.

This is the meaning of the Lord's Prayer. He waits on prayer. The cursing of the fig tree had a direct bearing on the house of prayer. Again, the house of prayer is people.

Prayer is the greatest power, privilege and asset of mortal life. It changes nations and is a more powerful resource than any political office. Properly used, it can alter the course of history, heal the sick. It can even raise the dead.

This was the point made by throwing over the tables in the temple. It was to fix the problem. It was to restore prayer power to the people. Is it not now high time to throw over the profligate activity and clean our own house? Otherwise, have we not made our temple—in like manner— into a den of thieves?

The Jewish Sanhedrin protested and demanded to know why he was turning over the tables.

"By what authority doest thou these things?
and who gave thee this authority?"
(Matt. 21:23)

They were saying, in essence, "Who do you think you are coming into our domain to do these things?

Now he had done it! Not only did he symbolically, metaphorically and physically curse the law, but the whole religious system. In turning over the tables, he was going after the truth of what truly ruled the Sanhedrin. This action was also to expose and demonstrate who was the god of the priests. It had become patently clear their real god was Mammon—in other words money. Jesus had overturned their god and that was it. Now for certain they had to kill him.

Had they known their own scriptures, they would not have erred, for they would have recalled the words of Jeremiah the prophet.

"Behold, the days come, saith the Lord, that
I will make a new covenant with the house of
Israel, and with the house of Judah:
    Not according to the covenant that I made
with their fathers in the day that I took them by
the hand to bring them out of the land of Egypt;
which my covenant they brake, although I was
a husband unto them, saith the Lord"

(Jer. 31:31-32)

Several days earlier on the road before entry to the city, Jesus wept. He wept because he knew that complete destruction was to come upon them and their city. They did not discern the signs of the time of their visitation which was spoken before by the prophets.

Now, in two days' time would come the Passover festival. It was to be a joyous celebration, but Jesus wept.

The momentum of the triumphal entry into the city, the cursing of the fig tree, and the fracas in the temple would cascade giving way to his detractor's unbridled hatred. They began accusing him of serious crimes and sedition against the state.

Things were about to get complicated and spin out of control, but it was God who was in control.

Chapter 8

OUTSIDE THE CAMP

"The high priest carries the blood of animals into the Most Holy Place as a sin offering, but the bodies are burned outside the camp. And so Jesus also suffered outside the city gate to make the people holy through his own blood. Let us, then, go to him outside the camp, bearing the disgrace he bore"

(Heb. 13:11–13)

A t this point we have to leave the narrative of Jesus' final days on earth briefly to investigate several significant details and terms that play into the importance of the overall message. Rest assured that the slight detour is well worth the experience and that we'll return to Jerusalem shortly.

Before pressing on to the last two days of Jesus life in the narrative, it is extremely important to understand the meaning of *the camp*. Few have sought to know the meaning of the term, but it has serious implications in terms of understanding the full biblical text, and the ability to grasp the where, how, and why Jesus was crucified. The critical implications of his death will be better understood once there is firm grasp on the meaning of *the camp*.

The camp is the context for understanding the very location of Jesus death. Where did Jesus actually die? He died outside the camp. This is what is written in the book of Hebrews.

> *Let us, then, go to him outside the camp,*
> *bearing the disgrace he bore*

As has been suggested, tradition is the enemy of the truth, but it is not just that tradition is contrary. The power of tradition has also blurred the truth and obstructed where the real location of Christ's death took place. And it is supremely important to know the purpose for the biblical directive to go outside the camp. Christian tradition has clearly replaced the actual biblical record with myth. Consequently, the twisted trick has insinuated itself into human history, leading people away and astray and from knowing the most sacred and holy site on the planet.

WHERE ON EARTH WAS CHRIST CRUCIFIED?

The answer to the *what, where*, and *why* will lead to a greater depth of understanding and a tremendous payoff into the full and complete knowledge of Christ's death.

The answer to the question of where is important because knowing *where* he died leads to *how* he died— and then the *why* he died. Most Christians believe, unequivocally, that his death relates to the forgiveness of sin, but they are still missing and overlooking a critical aspect of why he died. A significant part.

I can already hear the screaming. The acrimony of the religious Christians cannot be silenced.

"It is not important where he died only why he died!"

This is, of course, a religious reaction. It is also intellectual laziness, an evasion to digging deeper into discovering the truth—in this case a most important truth.

Yes, why he died is the point, but knowing where and how he died is crucial because it leads to a more complete understanding of the why he died. There is a fuller meaning to the why when the where and the how is uncovered.

> "And ye shall know the truth, and the truth shall make you free"
> **(John 8:32)**

The understanding of the biblical directive to go outside the camp is not a superficial. It is an important directive. Let us take pains to know the deep meaning. Bear with me on this little detour and we'll return to our narrative once we get things sorted out.

Where Jesus died leads to a vitally important part of his overall mission in the salvaging of the human race. If that were not the case, the powers of darkness would not have gone to such great lengths pointing the world in the wrong direction. In addition, they would not have taken such great measures to have filled the void with tradition, myths, and falsehoods. We are instructed to go outside the camp. Just how is this to be accomplished? How do we cooperate with the biblical directive?

Every year tens of thousands of people flock to Israel in order to visit the city of Jerusalem. The deep longing to walk in the footsteps of Jesus is a powerful incentive. Jerusalem is a magnet which draws the multitudes. But many of the places they go to identify with the life of Jesus and to draw close to him are just plain wrong.

I do not begrudge sincere people who love God and want to draw closer to him. Their heart is right, but their head is somewhere else.

A STEP IN THE WRONG DIRECTION

The Lord God looks at the heart for sure, but these poor folks are being sold a bill of goods even though they have sincere hearts. The misstep in this matter short circuits a tremendous blessing and a critical and important element for spiritual growth. Frankly, they are being robbed.

> *Let us, then, go to him outside the camp,*
> *bearing the disgrace he bore*

This scripture is important; however, is not taken seriously by the multitudes of people who flock to Jerusalem each year seeking to draw closer to God. Perhaps the reason is that going outside the camp means there is a price to pay, and that price is that of bearing his reproach.

Who wants to go against the tide? When the multitudes follow a tradition and the tradition is shown to be contrary to the truth, there is conflict. Conflict is painful. When Jesus was killed outside the camp, it was painful and shameful. If we are to go outside the camp with him, we should understand there will be reproach. Yet it is the price to be paid in order to draw closer to the Lord. Walking in the footsteps of Jesus is not visiting *supposed* holy sites, it is bearing his reproach. The reproach will come from the religious world which holds to their tradition(s).

Hebrews 13:13 is the key to the exact location where Jesus died. Nevertheless, the real meaning is ignored and tradition takes over. Bearing his reproach means going outside the camp. And going outside means it will invariably go against tradition. If tradition is the enemy of truth, then this means there is a battle. It means conflict. It means drama. It means war.

If only the religious would stop and take a look! But there is another important reason to find what it means to go outside the camp. Just as there is honor and friendship in suffering with him outside the camp, there is also healing and deliverance from spiritual blindness.

The healing is to be had outside the camp. Let us go outside the camp. It is outside the camp where there is deliverance from the ignorance that comes from traditionalism. God meets us there and the scales come off. We begin to see clearly outside the camp.

LAYING THE AX TO THE ROOT

In the fourth century AD, Helena the mother of Constantine had a dream in which she allegedly saw what she thought was the very place where Jesus was crucified, buried and rose again. She convinced her son, the Emperor, that the site was in the western part of the old city of Jerusalem.

Consequently, because of her dream, she convinced her son to build a church on that very spot to commemorate the most important of all events. Who would argue the death of Jesus was not the most important single event of all time? Anyone? And it was at that spot, indicated in her dream, where they (the Greeks) would end up building the Church of the Holy Sepulchre.

THE CHURCH OF THE HOLY SEPULCHRE

It took some ten years to build the Church of the Holy Sepulchre. It was intended to be the replacement for the Jews' temple which had been destroyed by the Romans in 70 AD. It was to be so spectacular that it would endure for countless centuries and would become, at least in their minds, the very center of the Earth.

Indeed, the edifice is still standing seventeen centuries later. Inside the church, the ancient worship rituals still continue to take place. Indeed, it is easy for religious traditionalists to consider the Church of the Holy Sepulchre a great tribute to Helena and Constantine, her wonderful ennobled son.

The problem is that, according to Jewish history and specifications, the Church of the Holy Sepulchre was not outside the camp. If the biblical directive is to go outside the camp, then there is a problem. If you go to the Church of the Holy Sepulchre, it is not outside the camp where Jesus died. It would have been *inside* the camp.

If only Helena and her son Constantine had known the scriptures, they could have spared the world a great deal of trouble. The fact of the matter is the building of the Church of the Holy Sepulchre has caused a great blindness. What has come from the grave error is a kind of confusion persisting through the centuries and morphing into a serious religious tradition. It has kept people from considering the meaning of *outside the camp.*

We are directed in the book of Hebrews to go outside the camp where Jesus suffered and died.

The Church of the Holy Sepulchre does not qualify as being outside the camp, so the location of the church as a landmark is simply inaccurate; it is not even biblical. The sad fact is that Catholics believe the Church of the Holy Sepulchre to be the sacred location of the death, burial, and resurrection of Jesus. This means billions—not *millions* but billions—of people who purpose to walk in the footsteps of Jesus are unable to do so. Still ardent traditionalists, when faced with this, will question if this matters.

Yes, it matters. It matters a great deal.

Thousands upon thousands of sincere pilgrims are spending extraordinary sums of money only to be being deceived as they seek to walk in the footsteps of Jesus. They come to Jerusalem taking the stroll on the Via Dolorosa [the way of grief or the way of the cross] all the way to the fabled Church of the Holy Sepulchre.

Along the famous six-hundred-meter roadway there are the purported stations of the cross. The fifteen stations of the cross are places—falsely established— believed to be where Jesus stopped to catch his breath and rest as he carried the cross. However, the many stopping points only embellish the myth that this was the way Jesus walked and where he would ultimately die.

The Via Dolorosa ends at the Church of the Holy Sepulchre. The truth is some clever genius figured out a way to funnel people along the supposed footsteps of Jesus all the way to the Greek Ordained Church. This is neither history nor theology, this is marketing. What a sad and tragic manipulation of human emotion and ignorance.

There are huge biblical problems with the tradition of both the famous walkway and the long enduring Church of the Holy Sepulchre itself.

We are going through this exercise to see how easily people are taken in and deceived by religion.

THE TRUTH WILL SET YOU FREE.

The Greek church has stood there for seventeen centuries. To the religious world, it stands as a monument. It is a testimony and so called physical proof to the veracity of the whole Helena story. Who can argue with what you see? Erect a monument, couch it in the institution and heritage of the Greek Orthodox Church, and many centuries later, it has taken root as "the truth".

It's really not true, but who can argue with the reputation and integrity of the institution of the Greek Orthodox Church, or the Catholic Church? Especially when there sits such a magnificent and enduring monument. It screams of the story's apparent authenticity and credibility? Who would go to such lengths to deceive the world? Yet it is not true. While the carefully crafted pathway and the remarkable church have long endured, the legend it has created is simply false.

One wonders what Jesus would do in the face of such a pervasive myth—and it is a myth. How might he approach such a mountainous tradition as the Church of the Holy Sepulchre?

"Jesus answered and said unto them, Verily
I say unto you, if ye have faith, and doubt
not, ye shall not only do this which is done to
the fig tree, but also if ye shall say unto this

mountain, be thou removed, and be thou cast
into the sea; it shall be done"

(Matt. 21:21)

—

"But he answered and said, every plant, which
my heavenly Father hath not planted, shall be
rooted up."

(Matt.15:13)

If God twice destroyed the Jewish temples because they
were not proper representations of his kingdom, then God will
also uproot and destroy traditional institutional Christianity
which also does not represent him. This should be interesting! It
may happen in our lifetime.

THE PROTESTANT MYTH

In addition to the myth of the Greeks as to the location of Jesus
death, the Protestants have their own version. Protestants hold to
a different view for the location of Christ's death, but in actuality,
it is just another myth. Their preferred location is at the so called
Garden Tomb.

The Protestants believe that just north of the Damascus
gate [about two hundred yards north] is a garden where they
believe Jesus was killed and buried. It is called the Garden Tomb.

Remember, *where* leads to *how*… and how to why.

The Garden Tomb is a real place, but it too is a myth that
has evolved into a religious tradition, one that has a vise like grip
on the world of Protestant believers. It is a powerful tradition.

It is powerful, because there are certain geographical features in the area that can be used to provide people with tangible proof of the location's supposed authenticity. When people become persuaded and convinced to accept the explanations surrounding the so called physical proofs, an emotional experience is triggered.

In fact, for those coming to Jerusalem—and especially the Garden Tomb—it is an unforgettable experience, but not for its historic value. It is the emotional experience that is unforgettable.

They genuinely believe—and it is because the emotions have been stirred—that this must be the real place. They become convinced by what they see (and then feel). But if only their eyes could be opened to the true facts, they would learn that tradition is the enemy of the truth. It is quite an eye opener. In fact, it is mind numbing.

The people come either weeping, praying, filming and conversing about what they think is the most historic spot in all the world, or they leave weeping. Yet it is all a myth. Yes, it is a real place alright, but it is not the true place where Jesus died.

Again, God sees the heart of the faithful, but was the Garden Tomb really the actual site?

Not a chance!

Please believe me. Again, I am not deriding people and believes, but the Garden Tomb was *not* where Jesus was killed nor buried. Nor was it the spot where he rose from the dead.

Remember, if we cannot establish where, then we cannot establish how, and finally the why. The full and total meaning for why he died has been left short of a most powerful spiritual reality; that reality is on the back burner, but it must come to the forefront of our faith.

Nevertheless, try telling that to a person emotion- ally charged by their belief or one who has made his living as a tour guide or even a minister. Think about the pastor who has made many trips along with his congregational members teaching the Garden Tomb as the actual biblical place where Jesus died.

Just try telling them that they are gravely mistaken. They will fight you tooth and nail. They may even go as so far to accuse you of speaking for the Devil; I have had people say this to my face. This is what to expect when you go outside the camp!

Those most caught in the amber of tradition are unlikely to ever embrace the truth. They would sub- consciously reason that their reputation was at stake. They would have the same reaction and problem as the Sanhedrin had during Jesus' day. Their authority would be at risk, their ego at stake. Solomon was right; there is nothing new under the sun. Tradition is the enemy of truth.

These poor folks are so heavily invested in their views that there is no turning back. Imagine the embarrassment, if the truth be known. After all the time having been looked to as the authority and now having to admit the truth. What a difficult situation for those who claim to be in the know

Jesus said it best:

"Let them alone: they be blind leaders of the blind. And if the blind lead the blind, both shall fall into the ditch"

(Matt. 15:14)

The deeply rooted traditional beliefs are the same problem Jesus faced in his confrontations with the religious authorities of his day. This is why he cursed the fig tree.

They said to him:

"Why do thy disciples transgress the tradition
of the elders? for they wash not their hands
when they eat bread.
 But he answered and said unto them, why
do ye also transgress the commandment of
God by your tradition?"

(Matt. 15:3)

As it was then, so it is today. After consuming and digesting
the body of this information, foundations will be rocked and
senses shocked. In fact, there may even come the temptation to
go to Israel to get first- hand experience—and what an education
it would be. Go to the Garden Tomb, and it will become evident.
The masses are following the blind guides. No wonder John the
Divine when he saw the Great Harlot of Babylon was awe struck.

"And upon her forehead was a name written,
Mystery, Babylon The Great, The Mother of
Harlots and Abominations of the Earth. And
I saw the woman drunken with the blood of
the saints, and with the blood of the martyrs
of Jesus: and when I saw her, I wondered with
great admiration"

(Rev. 17:5–6)

So then let us do this. Let us try to understand what it means
to go outside the camp. Let us go outside the camp where Jesus
died, for the directive to go outside the camp has tremendous
spiritual significance. We are instructed by biblical authority to

go outside the camp where Jesus died. And in doing so we will be able to see how tradition blinds from the truth.

Chapter 9

THE CIRCLE IS THE CAMP

ℰ∘ℰ

Several hours south of Jerusalem by car is a notable location called the Pillars of Solomon. It is located near the city of Eilat near the southern tip of Israel. It is not a site normally visited by tourist because it is far off the beaten path of most guided tour destinations. But the site is important because there stands a model or replica of the Tent of Meeting.

The Tent of Meeting was the mobile temple of God. It was used when the Hebrews were making their forty-year wilderness journey from bondage in Egypt to the Promised Land. God had instructed Moses to build a tent wherein he would meet with him; hence the Tent of Meeting.

In those days, accompanying the tent was a cloud that would descend over the tent. The cloud manifestation was unprecedented. The cloud was the physical presence of God, or the *shekhinah* [glory of God].

When the cloud would move, the people would follow. When the cloud came to stop and rest on the tent, the people would also stop and rest. When it moved again, they would move with it.

The Tent of Meeting had within it the ark of the covenant. Inside the ark of the covenant were the Ten Commandments, a jar of the manna, and Aaron's rod that budded. The Ten Commandments were handed down by God through the proxy of angels and were a testimony of his perfect will.[8] The manna was the supernatural food he fed them with in the wilderness. The jar of manna was a reminder of his supernatural provision in the wilderness. Aaron's rod that budded was a reminder of God's sovereign choice for who would officiate in the priesthood.

Each of these items were supernaturally derived and manifested by Jehovah/God. They were the testimony of his presence, his reality. They were a sign of his special favor and care for the Hebrews.

In addition, the lid of the ark of the covenant was called the mercy seat. Over the top of the mercy seat were two cherubim whose wings stretched across the *mercy seat*, and touched each other. The ark of the covenant was holy and it was placed inside the Tent of Meeting in the Holy of Holies.

This whole construction was unique and was only given to the Hebrews. They were his special covenant people. No other people on earth ever had had God's presence with them. The ark faced toward the east as though Jehovah God was looking eastward from inside the Tent of Meeting. From God's point of view, he was looking out through the opening in the tent.

Immediately to the east of the Tent of Meeting was the environs of the tribe of Judah. Each tribe was given a segment of the camp which was inside a circle circumscribed and enclosing all twelve tribes. It was like a clock with each tribe having a five-minute segment of the clock.

The circle was the camp.

It was as though, from God's point of view, from inside the Tent of Meeting, he was looking east. Immediately east he would be seeing the environs of the tribe of Judah, all the way to the perimeter of the circle.

This is a critical point to keep in mind in locating and actually pinpointing, thirteen hundred years later, where Jesus would be killed. It would be based on the circle which was the camp.

His vision from inside the tent over the mercy seat would have extended some two thousand cubits all the way to the *altar of the red heifer* which was just outside the circle. The circle; again, was the camp.

The two thousand cubits was the radius of the circle which encircled the whole of the Hebrew nation. Each of the twelve tribes of Israel was designated a piece of the pie or clock if you will. So then each tribe had a five-minute slice of the pie. The tribe of Judah had the slice that was directly east of the Tent of Meeting. And just outside the environ of the tribe of Judah there was the altar of the red heifer. Once again, that altar was outside the camp or outside the circle.

Again, God from inside the Tent of Meeting was facing east.

In the scripture, when it was said they brought the judgment in the face of God, it meant that they brought it before God who was facing eastward from (the ark of the covenant) his residence inside the Tent of Meeting.

Look at the scripture in the book of Numbers concerning the altar of the red heifer.

> "And ye shall give her [the red heifer] unto Eleazar the priest, that he may bring her forth without the camp, and one shall slay her before his face"
>
> **(Num 19:3)**

Then again, when it came to numbering the people for taking a census, God was facing eastward as though he was watching the activity of numbering. (Please refer to the book of Numbers Chapter 19 for more of an explanation for the term *in his presence.*)

When God looked out from inside the Tent of Meeting, his point of view would have gazed out over the tribe of Judas's environs. His vision would have extended some two thousand cubits to the perimeter of the circle (the camp) and beyond to altar of the red heifer.

So, there were three altars of the temple. The *altar of burnt offering* just immediately outside the entrance into the tent, and the *altar of incense* located nearby.

In addition, two thousand cubits east—a little over a half mile away—just beyond the circumference of the camp, was the third: the altar of the red heifer.

It is important to remember that the book of Hebrews was written to the Jews. When it was recorded, "Let us, then, go to him outside the camp, bearing the disgrace he bore," every Jew in the first century would have known what and where the camp was in those days. Today, it is virtually unknown. buried as it is under centuries of religious tradition.

KING DAVID SET UP THE CAMP

When King David came into the area and conquered the Jebusites to establish the holy city of Jerusalem (Jerusalem was then the "City of David") around one thousand BC, he used the same measurement of the two-thousand-cubit radius of the circle which Moses utilized. Moses in drawing the circle which defined the camp started inside the Tent of Meeting from which to draw his radius. King David drew the radius from a point inside the temple.

King David imposed the circle, over his own city Jerusalem, but now from the fixed and stationary temple. The circle had the same radius as in the wilderness days with the Tent of Meeting, and when the circle was drawn over the city it defined the camp. It was with this understanding the term the camp was used in Hebrews 13:13.

Let us, then, go to him outside the camp...

During the time of Jesus, the camp of Israel had already been fixed encircling the city of Jerusalem for over one thousand years. Everyone in the days of the first century knew what, and where the camp was even though today, two thousand years later it remains obscure. Today, the term the camp is just figure of speech, but in reality it has tremendous spiritual significance. However, it is virtually ignored as having any contemporary meaning, because people opt for religious traditionalism as opposed to the scriptures.

When there is a biblical directive to go outside the camp, it should be clear it meant outside the circle.

This eliminates the Church of the Holy Sepulchre for certain because it would have been *inside* the circle. The distance from inside the Jew's temple to the Church of the Holy Sepulchre would have been well short of two thousand cubits. In this calculation it is evident that had the people of the fourth century been careful to know the meaning of *outside the camp* they would not have allowed for the building of the fabled Church of the Holy Sepulchre.

But what about the Garden Tomb? Was the Garden Tomb area north of the city outside the circle of the camp as well?

Why do we need to know? Because it explodes the myth, and proves how easily people can be deceived,

> "For now we see through a glass, darkly; but then face to face: now I know in part; but then shall I know even as also I am known"
>
> **(1 Cor. 13:12)**

Chapter 10

FALSE FLAGS

༄

If the well-established tradition that the former Jewish temples stood at the same location as is presently occupied by the Dome of the Rock on the so called Temple Mount, then the Garden Tomb area would also fall inside the camp and be disqualified. Just as the Church of the Holy Sepulchre was a false flag so too the Garden Tomb.

This can be easily determined. By measuring from the golden Dome of the Rock as the center point of the circle and then scribing the circle with a two thousand cubit radius[9], the Garden Tomb falls inside the circle. So it is not difficult to see that the Garden Tomb, using this metric, is out of the question as being the legitimate place for Christ's death.

THE TEMPLE MOUNT ARGUMENT

Hold on! There is a serious question to consider. Here is the explosive question: was David and Solomon's temple really built up there on the Temple Mount? And was the second temple also built up there? This is a huge consideration. And no small argument either. In fact, the argument is a titanic collision between religious tradition as opposed to the real facts.

Tradition has it that the former temple(s) of the Jews were built on the location known as the Temple Mount. But why would locating the actual former temples location have any bearing on the true location of the place where Jesus was crucified? How does this work?

The precise location of the temple, in actuality, has a tremendous bearing on the true location of Jesus crucifixion.[10] There is incredible irony in this consideration, which is more than hypothesis it is fact.

It will take the rediscovery of the Jews temple(s) to accurately locate the place where the king of the Jews was crucified. In other words, it would take the Jews; who rejected Jesus as their Messiah, to actually find the very location of Jesus' death, burial and resurrection. Ironic isn't it?

THE JEWS' TEMPLE IS THE KEY

It is of critical importance to make sure to underscore that all sacrifices, polling, and census taking, and taxing of the people had to be done in the presence of God as he was looking out eastward through the doors from inside the Holy of Holies. His point of view was looking eastward from inside temple.

Once again, look at what was said after the two so called priests, the two sons of Aaron, had burned strange fire. The result was that they had to be slain. They had to be judged in front of the sanctuary which faced east. It had to be done in the presence of God.

> "And Moses called Mishael and Elzaphan, the sons of Uzziel the uncle of Aaron, and said unto them, Come near, carry your brethren from before the sanctuary out of the camp. So they went near, and carried them in their coats out of the camp; as Moses had said"
>
> **(Lev. 10:4–5)**

The two immoral sons of Arron were brought to the front of the Tent of Meeting as God was looking east-ward towards them. Then they were taken outside the camp to the alter of the red heifer.

What was the altar of the red heifer for?

The tribe of Judah was in God's line of view. God's point of view extended from the Holy of Holies out over the tribe of Judah all the way to the perimeter of the circle two thousand cubits away. And just beyond the circumference, he would have been able to see, in his line of view, the third altar of the temple—the altar of the red heifer. So the connection with the temple to outside the camp is obvious, thus the need to find the real site of the temple(s).

Sacrifices had to be seen, from God's point of view, and this was also true with regards to the altar of the red heifer. This location could be viewed from inside the temple looking out through the doors.

OUTSIDE THE CAMP

The tribe of Judah's designated location was just east of the Tent of Meeting, and after the city Jerusalem was established in the land, Judah took up its designated location again east of the temple. Just to the east of the boundary of Judah, outside the camp, was the third altar of the temple. The altar of the red heifer.

The altar of the red heifer was a little past two thou- sand cubits from the temple, but it was considered part of the altar system even though it was positioned outside the camp. It was the third altar.

It was often referred to as the *clean* place. In a more technical term the altar was called *Beth ha-Deshen* [the House of the Ashes]. The great prophet Ezekiel gave it the proper name when he called it the *outward sanctuary*.

> "Then he brought me back the way of the gate of the outward sanctuary which looketh toward the east; and it was shut"
> **(Ezek. 44:1)**

This altar was given a specific recognition. The recognition came when the glory of God retreated from the temple just before the temple was destroyed by the Babylonians. The glory of God retreated to the outward sanctuary.[11] Again the outward sanctuary was the location of the altar of the red heifer.[12]

Since there are instructions to go outside the camp where Jesus suffered and to bear with him in his shame, what significance was there to the altar of the red heifer?

The altar of the red heifer was set up outside the camp for a significant reason. Remember, it was east of the Tent of Meeting two thousand cubits away as though God was watching from his repose inside the tent of meeting looking eastward.

The altar of the red heifer was the location for a specific sacrifice.

One red female cow without spot or blemish was brought before the priests in the temple area first. Then it was led further eastward through the east gate of the temple, and past the tribe of Judah, all the way to the perimeter of the circle of the camp, and then outside of the circle. There outside the camp it was slain during the wilderness wanderings, and the same procedure was done afterwards when the temple was built.

It was to be burned to ashes with nothing remaining whatsoever; bone skin, entrails all were to be consumed by fire.

The altar and offering of the red heifer, ostensibly, was a sin offering—a cleansing of sin.

The ashes of the red heifer were to be utilized in a ceremonial way to purify those who were afflicted with sin or for those who were sick with diseases. This all had to happen outside the camp. It had to occur outside the camp because had the people come into the camp with their problems they would have defiled and have polluted the camp.

It was also outside the camp where the census was taken as well as the paying of taxes. The fig tree that Jesus cursed was also outside the camp.

All of these items resided outside the perimeter of the circle that represented the camp. But remember the census and tax collecting also occurred outside the camp near this Altar.

The altar of the red heifer located outside the camp—in symbolism—is certainly a representation of Jesus who was without spot or wrinkle or blemish and who was led outside the camp where he was slain.

> "We have an altar, whereof they have no right
> to eat which serve the tabernacle. For the
> bodies of those beasts, whose blood is brought
> into the sanctuary by the high priest for sin,
> are burned without the camp. Wherefore Jesus
> also, that he might sanctify the people with his
> own blood, suffered without the gate. Let us
> go forth therefore unto him without the camp,
> bearing his reproach"
> **(Heb. 13:10–13)**

Now that we have located the physical the camp in its historic context, the problem is it no longer exists. So what does it mean to go outside the camp? This is a serious question each person must ask of his and herself. If we are believers in Christ, then do we believe in him inside or outside the camp? This is a spiritual question.

There is a great difference between being religious and being spiritual. The difference is between actually knowing God as opposed to following after blind tradition and dogma.

To follow him outside the camp means persecution, rejection, humiliation, false accusations, and perhaps even death. Outside the camp is the offer of the fellow- ship of his suffering. Inside the camp means the honor of men, it means acceptance and the pride of success. It means the wealth of the world. Where do we go to meet Jesus? Inside the camp or outside the camp?

The greatest act of friendship extended by God is the fellowship of his suffering, and this occurs *outside* the camp.

Wherefore Jesus also, that he might sanctify the people with his own blood, suffered without the gate. Let us go forth therefore unto him without the camp, bearing his reproach.

Chapter 11

ZERO IN:
APPLES OF GOLD
IN PICTURES OF SILVER

ໝ

Can the spot where Jesus died be pin-pointed?
Some might well ask, "What difference does it
make now?"

Most of the world today believes that the former Jewish
temples were located in close proximity to the Muslim's
Dome of the Rock shrine. As has been indicated, all the
judgments of God had to take place in front of and to the east of
the Tent of Meeting and then later in front and east of the temple
in Jerusalem; in the face of God.

It stands to reason—which is to say logic dictates— that
the center of the camp would have been right where the Dome of
the Rock is situated, or at least nearby. But is this correct?

ANOTHER BLINDING TRADITION:
THE TEMPLE MOUNT

Today, countless tours with their guides lead people up to what they are told and is commonly believed to be the Temple Mount. They come to view the much heralded site where the whole world believes the two former Jewish temples (except for the Muslim of course) were situated. After all, why else is it called the Temple Mount?

They are also told that the eastern sealed gate is the gate that Jesus walked through, and that when he returns he will walk through it again. According to the common narrative, after he walks though the sealed gate, he will take his seat at the rebuilt third temple. The temple, it is told, will have been built near the very site where presently sits the Muslim Dome of the Rock shrine. This is the common narrative, and tradition.

Down below just to the west of the Dome of the Rock is the Wailing Wall, which today is noted by the Prime Minster of Israel, as the most holy place in all Israel. There at the Wailing Wall, throughout the day and into the evening, orthodox Jews pray to God that he might allow for the rebuilding of their third temple.

Two thousand years after the destruction of the second temple, and after being cast out of the land to the nations of the world, the Jews are back in their homeland. But there remains the final task of rebuilding a third temple.

Until the third temple is built, the centerpiece of the Jewish religion, their return, is not completed. In order to be fully restored, they must rebuild what was once destroyed by the Romans. So, the constant thought and prayer is for the rebuilding of the temple.

Now should they be able to rebuild their temple, the actual spot for the altar of the red heifer could be clearly located and established. The altar of the red heifer was the altar for the sin offering.

Once the temple is rebuilt all that would be needed to locate the altar of the red heifer would be to look out from inside the Holy of Holies, where the ark of the covenant had stood, through the two doors. Looking eastward and about a half mile and just due east of those doors would be the location of the altar of the red heifer.

The doors of the rebuilt temple would be as though one were looking through the scope of a rifle, *zeroing* in as it were. The doors, like a picture frame, would frame the exact place for the altar of the red heifer, and the exact place where Jesus was crucified.

Jesus had to completely fulfill what the red heifer sacrifice (for sin) could only do in part—because the red heifer was an animal sacrifice. He had to be killed near the altar of the red heifer. This is why he was killed east of the temple and why the Garden Tomb north of the city could not have been the most revered location. However, there are other reasons why the Garden Tomb must be disqualified—but first back to the temple.

No doubt if the temple could just be rebuilt, the most holy place where Jesus died would be found. And just to be clear it would not be at the Church of the Holy Sepulchre to the west nor the Garden Tomb area to the north, as the majority have mistakenly been led to believe.

The site of Jesus death had to be eastward looking out from inside the two doors of the Jews rebuilt temple in the face of God.

And if it were to be built, theoretically, at or near the Muslim Dome of the Rock, then framed in the doors of the temple would be the Mount of Olives. The Mount of Olives is directly east of the Dome of the Rock shrine.

But there is a major problem with this thesis, and it must be carefully considered.

What if the temples were not built on the Temple Mount?

What if the former temples of the Jews were not built up on the Temple Mount? This would change everything. The possibility for there to be a different site other than the Temple Mount itself, in most circles, is considered a preposterous notion. Who would propose such a thing? The whole world has been sold on the supposed Temple Mount. But is the well accepted site the real Temple Mount?

In an intellectual discussion, however, the proposition runs into severe headwinds. But what if the two former temples of the Jews were not built on the Temple Mount? What then?

If that were the case, then *all* calculations would be off. This would be a phenomenal and monumental problem in trying to establish the authentic site for Jesus' crucifixion because we need the doors to the Holy of Holies as a starting point.

But there is near universal consensus that the temples were once up there on the Temple Mount. This is the reason why they all want the third temple built at the same spot. Again, why else would they call it the Temple Mount? How can the whole world be wrong? So the foolish consideration that the former temples were built elsewhere is moot, right?

Let's look at some facts.

LOCATING THE HOLY OF HOLIES

When King David came to the general area today called Jerusalem, he saw a peculiar geological formation just due south of the walls which now surrounds the old city. The old city includes the Temple Mount. But in the time of David, the area surrounded by walls today, was not the Jerusalem of David's time. It was not Jerusalem of old.

David saw a narrow ridge about six hundred feet across and about one half to three quarters mile long. From an aerial view it had a crescent moon shape to it. This area has become known as the South East ridge and was the location of the City of David.

THE ACTUAL SITE OF THE CITY OF DAVID

At the southern portion of the southeast ridge, there was formerly a tall mount about four hundred fifty feet high, and it was called Mount Zion. (It is no longer present on the southeast ridge). The reason Mount Zion is no longer there is because in 180 BC Simon the Hasmonean cut down the mount and removed it. (The removal of Mount Zion is told in the film "Jerusalem and the Lost Temple of the Jews" and also in 1 Maccabees.)

The entire south east ridge was characterized by rugged cliffs rising up from the Kidron Valley on the east, and from the Tyropoeon Valley (valley of the Cheese mongers) on the west. The cliffs extended upward about three hundred feet.

The most remarkable feature of the area, however, was the water that flowed into the region via an under- ground spring. It was called the Gihon spring.

David saw this area as a perfect location for his city. He would eventually conquer the area and call it the City of David. The City of David was synonymous with Jerusalem. It *was* the Jerusalem of old.

Unfortunately, at the time, it was occupied by a Canaanite people called the Jebusites. They had built their city over the desirable piece of real estate for the same reasons David wanted it.

First it was a geographically well-fortified location, the terrain reaching upward several hundreds of feet and not easily conquerable. It was a natural fortification.

In fact, when Joshua, three hundred years earlier, tried to defeat the people he could not. It was a well- protected area, and a strategic location for David's capital city. As a military man this was the logical place to set up.

The second reason he wanted the city of Jebus was because of the water. Flowing down from Mount Scopus, about a mile away to the north, was a subterranean river that burst forth at the center of Jebus. It was like Old Faithful. When the waters from Mount Scopus reached the city, it shot upwards and carved out a shaft through the limestone rock. It later became known as *Warren's shaft.*

It was not just a small volume of water either, it gushed forth. This was the only water within five miles of the city. Today what is left of the gusher is called the Gihon Spring. It is still there, and in the time of David was the source of water which now flows through Hezekiah's tunnel.

The water meant David could take care of all the residents of his City of David and still have plentiful water for the daily needs of the temple and its priest- hood as well.

The Levitical priesthood needed an enormous amount of water every day for washing and also for the cleaning of the animals for sacrifices. In fact, 2 Chronicles 4:1–5 describes the *bronze laver* (a giant bowl) which held twenty-one thousand gallons of water and had to be filled every day. The laver was used to facilitate the needs of the priests. Notice it had to be filled every day, not once a week, but every day.

When David saw the natural fortification as a tremendous protection along with the enormous volume of water flowing into the area, he set about to conquer the city of Jebus from the Jebusites. Eventually he prevailed, and Jebus became the City of David—the Jerusalem of old.

The actual City of David was only re-discovered about one hundred and fifty years ago and today it is a well-attended tourist attraction. The City of David is about two hundred yards south of the what is commonly called today the Temple Mount.

But what sense did it make if the daily needs of the temple required twenty-one thousand gallons of water and would have had to be hand delivered from the Gihon Spring up several hundred yards away to the so called Temple Mount? Twenty-one thousand gallons' daily mind you—or almost *eighty-eight* tons of water. Just think about that.

David's City (Jerusalem) could be well fortified and protected by high ridges, and the water was so abundant right there next to his city. Why build the temple any other place then within the City of David?

In addition, the water actually gushed and shot upwards. There was no need to lug the water up to the temple hundreds of yards away. It was delivered right to the door. Why build the temple several hundred yards away at the so called Temple

Mount? It would make no sense especially not to a military man like King David.

And with the water shooting upwards, collecting it for the needs of the temple was a certain convenience.

It was a no-brainer as to where the temple would and should be built.

The temple(s) of the Jews were not built on the so called Temple Mount. Not only do the scriptures in the Old Testament confirm this fact, but common sense clearly dictates that they were built over the City of David. It was built just south of what today is called the Temple Mount.

But there is even more evidence that conclusively proves where the Jews former temples were located; a plethora of evidence. There are so many facts that add to this argument that it is best to watch the film "Jerusalem and the Lost Temples of the Jews."

But how in the world has the idea of the current Temple Mount be so far off?

Chapter 12

THE GIANT MISSTEP

৩৽৻

How is it even remotely possible that the whole world has it wrong? How could it be that, after two thousand years, the massive bias is so far from the truth?

When one stops to consider the many millions upon millions of pilgrims that have visited the holy land and have been taught that the temple(s) of the Jews were built at or near the Muslim Dome of the Rock, it is bewildering, but this is the view that most hold. Yet this is not only the prevailing view, it is the *overwhelming* view. And this is a view one dare not tamper with lest he be treated as a pariah.

City of David

Today, the Temple Mount is the source of tremendous political conflict, and it is because all parties, Muslims, Jews, and Christians alike, hold it with great reverence. It seems a day does not pass without some kind of collision between these warring factions, and the media is continually reporting on the explosive outcomes.

The Jews are so deeply passionate about the Temple Mount that every single day of the week they gather at the Wailing Wall beseeching God to bring about some kind of miracle which would allow them to rebuild their temple formerly destroyed by the Romans. And the Muslims are far from being dispassionate— that is a massive understatement. They stand ready to fight to the end, ensconced in a deeply held religious fervor over that which they claim is their own.

Since the time of Rabbi Isaac Luria (1534–1572), the Jews have been taught that the Wailing Wall was the outer western wall of their temple square (the site for both the temple of Solomon and the second temple of Zerubbabel).[13] They believe, wholeheartedly without a single doubt, that the temples were built just above the Wailing Wall and somewhere near the Dome of the Rock shrine.

For at least four centuries, they have been coming to the Wailing Wall to offer prayers to God that he might grant them access to rebuild their temple up at the site of the Muslim Dome of the Rock. Thousands upon thousands of written prayers are wedged into the cracks of the Wailing Wall, begging God to let them rebuild. But so far God has been silent.

All the encyclopedias and historical references support the bias and have been built on this premise. It is so pervasive that, to think otherwise, is nigh unthinkable! So then how can this be?

Why is this view so mistakenly wrong and such an enormous miscalculation? How can this possibly be such a grave error?

If the irony that it will take the Jews and their temple to locate the very spot where Christ was killed, then it makes sense that the removal of this great mountain of confusion, this giant misstep, would be the remedy for the situation. For there is no doubt—embedded as it is in historical cement—is the prevailing view that the temples of the Jews were firmly planted atop the violently contested Temple Mount. What a dilemma! But do we have the real history?

> "Be thou removed and be thou cast into the sea"
>
> **(Mark 11:23)**

Let's take a closer look at the history of Jerusalem to get a clearer picture of the why and how of this giant misstep.

First of all, the Jerusalem of today resembles not at all the Jerusalem of the time of King David circa

1000 BC. The walls surrounding the old city and the Temple Mount today are not those of the Jerusalem of those days. The real old city of Jerusalem was the City of David. The City of David was synonymous with the city of Jerusalem. They were one and the same.

The City of David/Jerusalem is several hundred meters south of the southern wall of the commonly one hundred and fifty years ago. But even with the archeological rediscovery of the City of David, the prevailing view and supposed location of the Temple Mount had been firmly established for many centuries.

WHERE THE TREE FALLS

One of the great proverbs of Solomon is "where the tree falls that is where it lies" (Eccl. 11:3).

And this is certainly applicable to the issue of the Temple Mount and the conundrum of where the temples were actually built.

The idea of this scripture is that many issues in life are weighty in nature. The proverb paints a picture of a tree as a metaphor of this fact. A tree is very heavy, so if one were to cut it down and had made a mistake in calculating where it would fall, there would be the problem of dealing with moving it from where it fell.

It would take a great deal of work to chop up the fallen tree into pieces and remove it. So it is with the case of the Temple Mount dilemma. Where the tree falls that's where it lies. Yet even though the City of David had been rediscovered one hundred and fifty years ago, the tree has been laying there still after four centuries. But a simple logical consideration should cause one to take pause about at least the *possibility* that maybe, just maybe, the temples were not built on the so called Temple Mount, but rather in the City of David. "Where the tree falls that's where it lies!"

BUT THE MOMENTUM FOR THE CONFUSION COMMENCED LONG AGO

How did the confusion begin? Let us go back and exhume and then review the evolution of the history that caused the giant misstep and what has resulted in today's prevailing bias.

The beginning of the confusion commenced after the destruction of the first temple. This was some six hundred years before Christ. The Jews had been carried off to Babylon around 600 BC. Then after seventy years in bondage, they were allowed to return and rebuild their temple.

But first they rebuilt the walls surrounding the temple square and, astonishingly, according to the book of Nehemiah, they accomplished the feat in just fifty-two days.

> "So the wall was completed on the twenty-
> fifth of the month Elul, in fifty-two days"
> **(Neh. 6:15)**

Most people who read the bible would never stop to ponder and thus consider this important fact of history. But this fact sheds great light on where the temple(s) formerly stood. It is a very significant historical fact.

There is simply no humanly way possible that the Jews could have laid both the foundations and then build back the walls surrounding the city in just fifty-two days. No way!

When the Jews returned from Babylon to Jerusalem, they merely gathered the massive rocks of the wall that had been knocked down and strewn in the Kidron Valley and put them back on their original foundations. These were the foundations which Solomon had laid centuries earlier. This took the Jews only fifty-two days. No problem.

So what? Here is the point.

There was only one other time in Jewish history when the walls were torn down subsequent to when the Jews returned from Babylon. This took place in 63 BC. When Jerusalem was invaded by the Romans under the direction of Pompey.

The walls were knocked down, but they were immediately put back in place, and for that to happen there was no time to lay down new foundations. The stones that formed the walls were put back on top of the old original foundations laid down by Solomon. Just as the Jews replaced the walls in fifty-two days on their return from Babylon on top of Solomon's foundations so did Pompey do the same.

Those walls, replaced by Pompey, remained for over one hundred years until the Romans again invaded Jerusalem in 70 AD at the leadership of Titus, and destroyed the city and the walls.

Until the time of the Roman destruction of Jerusalem, in 70 AD the walls had remained intact for over one hundred years.

So what is the point?

The stones that make up the foundation stones around the Temple Mount today were laid there by the Romans under Herod. This was at least forty years after Pompey. How could stones that formerly formed the walls of the city after Pompey's restoration, and placed on Solomon's original foundations end up on top of Herod's foundations?

This one fact, in and of itself, proves that the current so called Temple Mount was not the site of either the Solomon temple nor the Zerubbabel temple.

This simple lost historical fact is the beginning for understanding the evolution of the misstep.

MORE CONCERNING THE FOUNDATION STONES

When the Romans came and destroyed the city and the temple in 70 AD, according to Jesus' prophecy, they tore down the walls even down to the foundations. Nothing was left.[14]

Jesus prophesied that, in the future, the Temple of Jerusalem would be destroyed and that its destruction would be so complete that not one stone would be left standing on top of another. His prophecy was fulfilled about forty years later when the Romans destroyed Jerusalem and tore down the Temple.

The destruction was so complete that even the foundations of the Temple were dug up. These facts are recorded in the writings of Flavius Josephus, an eyewitness and historian of the time who wrote about the destruction. This forecast was also recorded in the book of Matthew.

How is it, then, that there are still foundation stones (*Roman* foundation stones no less) today that undergird the walls that surround the Temple Mount? The answer is that what is called the Temple Mount is not the real Temple Mount.

THE NEXT STEP

The next step in exhuming the history and evolution which has led to the prevailing bias of the Temple Mount, occurred during the time of the Maccabees. This was circa 180 BC. It was at that time that Simon the Hasmonean (Simon was a Maccabee who had become the Jewish king and priest over Israel) took action by consent of the people.

His anger sprung from what the Syrian king (Antiochus IV) had accomplished when he desecrated the Jewish temple and seized the citadel of David atop Mount Zion. The citadel looked down on the temple area and was a strategic military vantage position.

Simon decided to not only tear down and rebuild the desecrated temple because it had become utterly unusable, but he also decided to cut down Mount Zion.

He never wanted an enemy to again gain the tactical advantage of the high ground of Mount Zion. This is recorded in the book of Maccabees. So Simon excavated Mount Zion. The task took three years. Jerusalem of old was getting a kind of topographical alteration and would become significantly changed.

Simon took the dirt from the excavated mountain and used it to build up and level out what would later come to be known as the Temple Mount. Prior to that episode, the area was a massive thirty-five-acre rocky formation with crags, uneven ridges and depressions. The dirt from the excavated Mount Zion was used to smooth out the highs and lows of the rocky terrain. It was made it into a level plateau.[15]

Remains of the massive rock formation mentioned by Flavius Josephus[16] is still peeking through the plateau. It is the visible remaining rock underneath the Dome of the Rock.

Then Simon proceeded to build a fort up there called the Baris to protect the temple from invaders who would approach and attack the city and temple from the north. Jerusalem was defended and secured, but later Herod, the great builder, would enhance and greatly enlarge the Baris fort and call it after his friend Mark Anthony. Thus it became known as the Antonia fortress. But what had this to do with the location of the proper Temple Mount?

Now that Mount Zion had been removed, there was no longer the landmark and high place to look down on the real location of the temple. Attention began, ever so slowly, to drift and shift some two hundred meters north of the original site.

ENTER HEROD THE GREAT

Herod like so many who come to power was a megalomaniac. When he married into the Hasmoneans kingly line, it was to gain political advantage and credibility with the Jews. He ended up murdering his Hasmonean wife, but to some extent, he was yet fearful of the God of the Jews.

Here is how he acquired religion and how it affected the Temple Mount.

When King David was gathering the resources for the first temple, he accumulated a tremendous fortune in gold and silver.[17] So much so that he ended up storing the massive treasure in the tomb he had built for when he would die.

When the evil Syrian king Antiochus plundered the temple many centuries later, he desecrated it, and Simon the Hasmonean eventually paid off Antiochus to never return again. He paid him with a significant amount of silver from king David's tomb.[17]

Later when Herod came to power, he learned of the payoff and sought to find King David's tomb. He was obviously tempted to find the gold and silver. When the tomb was located, two of his men were sent to procure the massive treasure. They drilled into the wall and placed their torches into the breech of the wall of the tomb to see what they could see. Immediately a powerful gout of flame shot out and killed the two men. Primitive minds did not know that, over a period of time, limestone puts out a gas. The flame ignited the gas causing the men to be instantly killed.[18]

Herod felt it was a serious warning by the Jewish God. As a result, in great dread, he determined to appease the "angry God of Israel." In an act of tremendous contrition and appeasement Herod greatly added onto the temple and then attached the temple to his enlarged Antonia fortress. The temple, henceforth, would become known as Herod's temple.

The whole temple complex began to take on a different configuration than the former Solomon and Zerubbabel temples. The face of Jerusalem was continuing to change.

THE REALLY BIG CHANGE

The most noteworthy alteration to the face of Jerusalem, however, came forty years after Jesus predicted what would come upon the Jewish nation. It all began in 66 AD.

> "Where then are those palaces? Where is the Temple where are the walls? Where are the defenses of the towers? Where is the power of the Israelites? Were not they scattered in different quarters over almost the whole world? And in their overthrow their palaces also were brought to ruin."
>
> **—Gregory of Nyssa**[19]

It was in 66 AD when the Jews entered into a civil war. The conflict broke out between the religious factions of the Pharisees and Sadducees. The war escalated, and the Romans tenth legion intervened to put down the conflict. But the entry of Rome into the conflagration only accentuated the trouble.

Soon, in only three and a half years, both the temple and the city would undergo a complete destruction. Jerusalem was devastated and raised to the ground by Rome.

The devastation was so profound that nothing was left of either the city or the temple. It was a complete destruction even down to the foundations. No one afterward could even recognize that a city had ever been there.

Eleazar who led the Masada revolt stated that all that was left of Jerusalem was the fortress of our enemy, which was the Antonia fortress, as recorded in the writings of Flavius Josephus.[20]

Over one million Jews were murdered, and the rest who were not killed either fled or were caught and sold into slavery. But sixty years later, the Jews were able to mount a revolt as they sought to regain their city. It was called the Bar Kokhba revolt. Nevertheless, the revolt did not succeed and was extinguished by the Roman emperor Hadrian.

Hadrian hated the Jews and their Hebrew religion and sought to eliminate this "horrible race" and their culture forever. He changed the name of Israel to Palestine and the name of Jerusalem to Aelia Capitolina.

Thus we see another step in the stepping stones toward the eradication of the knowledge of the true site of the Temple Mount. But there is more to the story.

ENTER CONSTANTINE AND HIS MOTHER HELENA

Several hundred years passed, and the Emperor Constantine came into power. This was in the fourth century. Constantine, the Christian, kept the tradition of Hadrian and forbade Jews from entering into Jerusalem. Consequently, there were few if any records kept by Jews of the true location of their former temple(s).

Then Constantine's mother, Helena, had a dream in which she envisioned a Christian church to be built on the west side of the city. It was later to be called the Church of the Holy Sepulcher.

The idea for the Church was that it would be the replacement for the Jews' holy temple(s). Now they dreamed the center of the earth would be a Christian church, instead of the Jewish temple. Helena and her son Constantine proceeded in changing the former Jewish city (albeit controlled by Rome) and would transform it into a Christian city. The Church of the Holy Sepulchre would be the centerpiece of the city.[21]

She also proceeded to build a Christian church (Church of the Holy Wisdom) up on the location where now sits the Dome of the Rock. Why? There is no direct written account of her motives, so it is mere conjecture, but it was probably because she considered the site as the location of the Jews' former temples.

She most likely wanted to memorialize the historic location albeit with a Christian church. This all occurred in the fourth century, but her actions in building a church up there established a precedent that set in motion the tradition for the area to be later known as the Temple Mount

OMAR SEALS THE DEAL

Several hundred years passed, and the Muslims took control of the city. In the sixth and seventh centuries, Muslims looked more favorably toward Jews than they do today.

When the Muslim caliph Omar came into town riding on his camel, he came with an attitude of respect toward both King Solomon and King David. The Muslims still held Solomon and King David with reverence, so Omar sought to locate where they had prayed.

At that time, the Church of the Holy Sepulchre, built by Helena and Constantine, had been standing for three centuries, but it still had a resident bishop there named Sophronius. He was the patriarch of Jerusalem.

Omar came to Sophronius to inquire if he would tell him where both Solomon and David prayed. Reluctantly, Sophronius gave into the petition of Omar—but only after Omar agreed to a deal. The deal was that he was not to allow any Jews back into the city. The Christians hated the Jews and did not ever again want them to rebuild their temple (all these facts can be substantiated by the Geniza letters[22] found in a synagogue in Cairo Egypt).[23]

So the religious authorities tried to conceal the truth of the location of the Jewish temple(s) and focus was continuing to shift towards what would become known as the Temple Mount.

BUT THEN AN ACCELERATION OCCURRED

Omar was told by Sophronius that the actual site of the temples was down by the Gihon spring. This was where Sophronius told him David and Solomon had prayed.

The Gihon spring was, of course, the location of the water supply that was utilized by the Jebusites. After King David conquered Jebus, he did the same for both the needs of the city and the daily needs of the priest- hood and temple service. When Omar went to the Gihon spring area to pray, he discovered many of the original stones from the walls and the temple that had been knocked down by the Romans. They were still laying there now for several hundred years.

He found one stone in particular that he thought was the stone upon which lay the Ark of the Covenant. He took that stone and carried it to the site which he had seen in a dream. That site is where the Al Aqsa mosque sits today; on the south end of the Temple Mount.[24]

In an act called a *Baraka* which means in the Muslim faith to *transfer*. He took the stone from the Kidron valley and transferred it to its present site where it became holy to the Muslims.

After this ritual, Omar took the remaining stones he found down in the Kidron Valley and used them to build the Al Aqsa mosque. Since the stones were associated with the Temple of Solomon, the Al Aqsa mosque became known as the new Temple of Solomon. Now the new Temple of Solomon was connected to the so-called Temple Mount. This is how it began to be called the Temple Mount. So then from the time of the seventh century, the site has become a holy site for Muslims even to this day.

But the idea of the Jews temple being up there is an enormous mistake. It is a miscalculation of history. And there is a general a lack of objective knowledge as to the events that shifted the attention form the Gihon spring and the City of David to the present Temple Mount.

Nevertheless, for several centuries, until the city was recaptured by the Christians (Jerusalem was recaptured in 1099), the idea of this being the real site of Solomon's temple and then the second temple had already become a deeply ingrained belief.

When the crusaders arrived in 1099, the idea of the area being the Temple Mount to them was unquestionable. To them it was a matter of fact. When the Franciscan priests ignorantly picked up the accepted notion, stemming from the false history, they just continued what had become a tradition and perpetuated what was false.

When they came up with the fallacious idea that Jesus was taken from the spot *thought* to be site of the Antonia fortress marched north outside the walls and onto an invented Via *Dolorosa* (the way of grief) another religious tradition was born and set in motion. All of this was of a religious convenience and a mythological invention which stubbornly persists to this day.

But the real problem of the tradition is that it perpetuates the mistaken idea that today's Temple Mount was the site of the Jews' temple, but it is a false history, and only added to the giant misstep.

THE MYSTICAL RABBI

After these events, along came Rabbi Isaac Luria in the sixteenth century, and he further exacerbated the false notion and false history. Luria was hailed as the greatest mystic of his time. He had many followers and evidently was able to convince the people that he could supernaturally identify people who were buried in unmarked tombs.

When identities of the departed became mystically claimed by Luria, the people would place stones on the tombs sympathetically identifying with those who had passed.

This strange practice was initiated by Rabbi Luria. In fact, the very act can still be witnessed in the famous movie Schindler's list. Jews who remained having been saved from the holocaust by Schindler give honor to him by placing small stones on his tomb. This is a practice that can be traced back to Rabbi Luria.

But the Rabbi also claimed that the Western Wall, or what came to be known as the Wailing Wall, was truly the outer wall of the Jews holy and venerated temple. It was because of his mystical practices and his strong following that the people were convinced in what he said.

This is how the practice of the Jews going to the Wailing Wall commenced. And while the Jews prior to this time prayed from the Mount of Olives facing west, now due to Rabbi Luria, they began to pray from the Walling Wall facing east.[25]

Yet the Wailing Wall is not the western wall of the former temples because all the walls of the temple were, as Jesus said, destroyed even to their foundations. The Wailing Wall, in reality, is the western wall of the fortress Antonia.

So the Western Wall is nothing more than the wall that was built up by Herod that supports all the fill dirt taken from Mount Zion. It is merely a retaining wall!

If you want to stand on Mount Zion today, go to the so-called Temple Mount and you can stand on it. It is all the excavated dirt taken from Mount Zion by Simon, and the walls, even the Wailing Wall, is nothing more than a retaining wall to hold back all the dirt. Strange world isn't it?

DR. MICHAEL AVI YONAH INFLUENCED THE WHOLE WORLD

There is one last thing that needs to be mentioned, which brings us up to date. The continuation of the false history that keeps the whole world in darkness as to the real location for the temples has been perpetuated by the colossal work of Dr. Michael Avi Yonah.

Doctor Yonah, a well seeming man, was a respected archeologist and historian at Hebrew University. He passed away in 1974, but not before completing his historic rendering of the city of Jerusalem in his scaled down model of the city of the first century. It is a major attraction for pilgrims visiting Jerusalem.

Today, thousands upon thousands of people visit the Jerusalem museum just to view the model. Not only that, but nearly every encyclopedia and Bible dictionary in the world—and certainly all the Jewish literature—contain pictures of his model. Its published presence is pervasive.

The very fact that he created a visual rendering of the city of the first century when no one else in the world had ever undertaken the task has given his presentation preeminence and great—yet unwarranted— credibility. It creates an indelible impression for all who are interested in inquiring about what the City of Jerusalem was like in the time of Jesus.

Here is Jerusalem as it was back then, before the Romans destroyed it; and who could argue? There was nothing in existence to compare with his rendering. His model was the only visual example and yardstick.

Up until the present, no one has challenged his views, nor his world famous model. But now that we are gaining a better understanding of the history of Jerusalem, it is time to revisit Yonah's findings.[26]

Where did Yonah find the information which allowed him to visualize and then conceptualize what the city had looked like in the first century? His task was certainly complicated, and he needs to be applauded and commended for at least stepping up to the challenge, but much of his visualization sprung from supposition based upon traditions and sketchy histories. Give him credit though, he tried and did his best.

As Jews were expunged from the land for many centuries, there was a paucity of written records. Yonah had to rely on Jewish verbal tradition, the writing of Flavius Josephus, and the records of the Greek Orthodox and Catholic churches.

However, in regards to the writing of Josephus, Yonah was very selective. He only used Josephus when Josephus supported his premise and preconceived bias. Otherwise Josephus was not consulted. A case in particular is the Antonia fortress.

Yonah's most glaring error and offense in the model is that of his presentation of the size of the Antonia fortress.

Josephus recorded, in his writings, that the Antonia fortress sat on a rock that was thirty-five acres and housed and garrisoned the Roman tenth legion. The Roman tenth legion was composed of six thousand men. But the Antonia fortress rendering of Yonah's historic model could have supported no more than a cohort.[27]

A cohort is only five hundred men, so Yonah's model of the Antonia is far too small for Josephus' description of it. As can be seen in this example, Yonah selectively edits and dismisses Flavius Josephus' written historical eyewitness account. He selectively ignores Josephus.

Yonah actually followed the mythological story created by the Franciscan priests of the twelfth century with regard to the alleged Via Dolorosa to build his premise. The Via Dolorosa was the supposed road Jesus took, carrying his pagan Roman cross on the way to where he would be crucified.

Yonah thus had to place the spot for his diminutive Antonia fortress—where supposedly Christ was whipped, beaten and the crown of thorns placed on His head—to the north and to the west of the walls that surround the Temple Mount.

He did this in error because there are paving stones in that area that were erroneously determined to be the pavement stones of the Antonia Fortress. In the view of the high churches, Jesus had to be beaten on those pavement stones. They believed those paving stones indicated where the Antonia Fortress once stood.

So following the lead of the high churches, those paving stones, he mistakenly determined and then extrapolated, must have been the very place of the Antonia Fortress. The Via Dolorosa invented by the Franciscan monks convinced him of this as a historic fact and certainty.

But those paving stones were placed there by Hadrian in 130 AD. One hundred years after Jesus' death. How could they have been the paving stones of the Antonia Fortress when they hadn't been laid down there for another hundred years?

Today there sits a Catholic church, the Ecce Homo Church (*Ecce Homo* meaning *behold the Man*), over those paving stones memorializing, erroneously, as the spot where Jesus was whipped.

Remember Yonah's model is the lens through which the world looks to visualize and format an idea of first century Jerusalem and thus the location for the temples. Yonah's colossal errors have continued to lead and point the world in the wrong direction.

What Yonah had presented in his historic model has become historical dogma, but it is a faulty lens, and none of this is true, but tragically it perpetuates the giant misstep and bias that actually prevents the Jews from rebuilding their third temple.

And for the Christians, it points in the wrong direction and the wrong place of the most holy site on earth. The actual place of Jesus' death, and thus obscures why that very holy place is so critically important.

All these factors, occurring over many centuries, in fact over millennium, have contributed to a massive illusory idea of the Temple Mount. The real truth is virtually imperceptible due to the rolling events over a great expanse of time, which human beings simply cannot grasp nor see.

Nevertheless, once the historical dots are connected, it becomes obvious and clear as to the real truth. And those who still adhere and cling to a history of Jerusalem as it has been erroneously presented are simply blinded and ignorant of the truth.

Only through the lens of the panorama of time and history can it be clearly seen that the delusion under which the Jews, Muslims and Christians so sadly labor is so remarkably false.

"It is the glory of God to conceal a thing: but
the honor of kings is to search out a matter"
(Prov. 25:2)

Chapter 13

LOCATING THE HOLY OF HOLIES

So then, with the approximate location of the temple(s) there is the challenge of finding the Holy of Holies. This is of vital importance. By discovering the exact location for the Holy of Holies, we can begin the reconstruction of the temple doors. Once that is accomplished, the doors would actually frame in the exact site of the altar of the red heifer. This would locate the actual place and location of the crucifixion of Jesus. The holy place of his death. The question is how can the Holy of Holies be determined precisely?

FALSE FLAG MISSTEPS

Just north of the Wailing Wall (the Wailing Wall is a portion of the Western Wall) there is a tunnel that follows the Western Wall north all the way to where the wall ends. It is called the Kotel. Inside the tunnel there is a location which faces the wall where people can be found praying They have been led to believe that this spot is right in front of the Holy of Holies, which in their thinking, would lay just behind the wall.

Again, I do not mean to belittle the people's faith, devotion, or their sincerity. I have also seen people praying and weeping over a stone in the Church of the Holy Sepulchre. The stone is erroneously believed to be the very stone upon which Jesus was lain after he died. Not so!

The people crying and praying over the supposed stone love God. I believe God accepts their contrition and reverence. I have also seen men and women weeping at the Garden Tomb when they go inside, believing this was Jesus tomb. The emotions take over, and fountains of tears flow.

In like manner, at the wall inside the Kotel, people are also weeping. The same as the other aforementioned instances, but again are these legitimate holy places? The answer is no, not one of them is.

But please remember, tradition is the enemy of truth.

And because people believe wholeheartedly that these are the actual historic sites, they attach sentiments and have emotional experiences. But an emotional experience is not a spiritual experience. This is an important fact because once an emotion is attached to a thought it becomes powerfully embedded in the soul. But the real facts support otherwise.

When it comes to finding the true location of the Holies of Holies, there are a few hurdles to clear. And because there are historic complexities, it takes a bit of leg work and research to uncover the true facts.

"It is the glory of God to conceal a thing: but
the honor of kings is to search out a matter"
(Prov. 25:2)

This is a scripture to be loved by students and researchers. God loves hiding mysteries, and he loves the searching out of those secrets.

One of the reasons people fall for pseudo-religious ideas, myths and false doctrines is due to the fact they simply do not study. It is so much easier to be spoon fed and just remain lazy and take the word of someone else. If they know five percent more than you, then they are an expert. This is how and why people get duped. We should rather be diligent and study.

THE ARK OF THE COVENANT, THE HOLY OF HOLIES, AND THE TEMPLE

The movie "Raiders of the Lost Ark" made famous the Jew's ark of the covenant. But in the real story, when the Babylonians destroyed the city Jerusalem, circa 600 BC, the ark was lost. Where the ark was taken is a grab bag of conjecture. No one knows for certain. Will the ark return for the third temple is also uncertain. But this we do know.

We know from the writing of Flavius Josephus that the temple had specific parameters and measurement. But first of all it should be noted that the Antonia for- tress that was butted up next to the temple complex was actually situated on a massive area. It was thirty- five acres according to Flavius.

However, in the well-known model of the city of Jerusalem (the model of first century Jerusalem is at the museum in Jerusalem) there is an inaccurate rendering of the Antonia fortress. In the model representation, the Antonia fortress is featured as a small building. The fortress in the model could have only contained about five hundred men.

But Josephus, an eyewitness, described the Antonia fortress as massive. It contained ten thousand men. It was the headquarters for the entire Roman tenth legion. A legion was six thousand men and then there were another four thousand that had to support that legion. So the Antonia fortress of Josephus was far larger than the ever popular and well accepted model at the Jerusalem museum.

These dimensions are very important to take into consideration. They will help locate the accurate location of the temple. This will lead to the discovery of the Holy of Holies.

According to Josephus, the Antonia fortress was built over a huge rock[28] which was some thirty-five acres. What can be seen of the visible remaining thirty-five-acre rock today is underneath the Dome of the Rock. The Dome of the Rock covers over what can still be seen of the thirty-five-acre rock.

The entire rock area was actually leveled out with fill dirt[29] and made into a plateau so that a fort could be built up there. The fort was originally built by the Jewish Simon the Hasmonean about 180 BC. The fort was called the Baris.

Simon took fill dirt and smoothed out the surface of the thirty-five-acre rocky area, so that he could build a fort up there to protect the northern flank of the temple. Ironically, the fill dirt came from the southern part of the City of David.

Today, there is no longer Mount Zion unless you visit the so called Temple Mount where you can stand on it. All the dirt up there came from the excavation of Mount Zion; albeit, they left the apex of the rock underneath the Dome of the Rock. The entire episode is recorded in the book of 1 Maccabees.

And if one views the south eastern ridge from the Mount of Olives—looking west to the location of the City of David— one can still see where the ridge was cut down. It was actually terraced down but the mountain (Mount Zion) is gone. It was amputated. This was the work of Simon and it took three years to excavate the fabled Mount Zion.

Later on, Herod the Great built onto the fort, vastly enlarging it, and it held the tenth legion consisting of ten thousand men. The walls that surround the area and encompass the misnamed Temple Mount were virtually the entire site of the Antonia fortress.

DETAILS DETAILS: THE MISSING ONE HUNDRED AND SEVENTEEN FEET

But not quite the *entire* site. And this is critical for finding the exact location of the temple and thus the Holy of Holies.

You must prepare yourself to think hard. The understanding of these details leads to the understanding of how God concealed the matter. It is time for the honor of kings to search out the matter.

During the time of Jesus in the first century, the southern end of the Temple Mount was shorter. About one hundred and seventeen feet shorter. The knowledge of this apparent discrepancy is not widely known. But it is a critical detail in pinpointing the actual location of the temple(s) and the Holy of Holies.

> "Jesus answered and said unto them, destroy
> this temple, and in three days I will raise it up."
> **(John 2:19)**

It was this statement by Jesus that pushed the Sanhedrin over the edge; it was why they accused him of blasphemy among other charges.

> "Then said the Jews, Forty and six years was
> this temple in building, and wilt thou rear it up
> in three days?"
>
> **(John 2:20)**

Ironically it will take the finding of the location of the Jewish temple and the Holy of Holies to rediscover where Jesus would eventually be murdered. It will take the rebuilding of the Jewish temple to find where Jesus was crucified. It will take the Jews to find where Jesus died! If that is not irony, then what is?

And the key to finding the location for the Holy of Holies which determines the doors, requires the exact knowledge of the actual length of the so called Temple Mount during the time of Jesus

Here are the important details.

After Simon the Hasmonean excavated Mount Zion. He tore down the temple of Zerubbabel (about 180 BC), the second temple, and then rebuilt it because temple had been so defiled by Antiochus IV that it was desecrated in Simon's eyes and unusable.

Simon torn down that temple and then had it rebuilt. Then the Maccabees led by Simon built the fortress called the Baris to the north up on what today is called the Temple Mount.

Then about one hundred and fifty years later, about the middle of the first century BC, Herod the Great built onto the temple and enlarged the Baris to an extraordinary degree. He dedicated the area and called it Fortress Antonia after Mark Anthony of Rome.

Herod was an Edomite genetically speaking. He married into the royal line of the Maccabees for political and credibility purposes. Afterward, he murdered his Jewish wife—needless to say, Herod was a politically power hungry megalomaniac. He nevertheless sought favor with the Jews and built onto their temple and its precincts. That is why, in some circles, the temple during Jesus time was referred to Herod's temple square by building two six hundred foot colonnades that stretched from the Antonia fortress over the western side of a mezzanine-plaza area all the way to the temple square.[30]

The colonnades stretching six hundred feet pro- vided a means to reach the Jews if an uprising were to take place in the temple area. Soldiers from the Antonia fortress would be dispatched over the colonnades to the temple area to put down any trouble.

The Jews, at that time, were notorious for fighting amongst themselves. Their religious beliefs became fractured and divided into two conflicting parties: The Pharisees and the Sadducees. They would often brawl in the temple area.

The festering ongoing conflict finally broke out into the civil war in sixty-six AD. The war escalated drawing in the Romans. The whole fracas eventuated into the massive Roman invasion and the total destruction of the city and the temple. It was the devastation Jesus had predicted during the last week of his life.

But in Herod's day, the animosity between the rival Jewish factions could be controlled. Troops could quickly be deployed from the Antonia fortress via the colonnades to control the activities in the temple only six hundred feet away.

But in calculating the length for the Temple Mount (falsely and erroneously known as the Temple Mount today) during the time of Herod (it was the Antonia fortress) the length was shorter.

So there is a problem measuring from the actual length of the southern wall today. During the first feet shorter.

During the time of Herod, it did not extend to where it stands today. Today of course over and above the southern end sits the Muslim Al-Aqsa Mosque. But the Mosque was not built until the seventh century AD and neither was the golden Dome of the Rock shrine.

The way it is known that the plateau's length was extended by one hundred and seventeen feet is due to a seam on the eastern wall that surrounds the thirty- five acres. The seam marks the place where the addition was made. The walls on both the west side and east side were extended one hundred and seventeen feet to its present position.

The addition to the entire area was made by Justinian in the sixth century AD. He needed additional acreage to build his great Nea church.

The Nea Christian church was huge and required more space (in the time of Justinian there was no Muslim Al-Aqsa mosque and no Dome of the Rock shrine). Justinian added onto the southern end of the area to accommodate the need for a larger area for his church. What is called the Temple Mount was extended. It was added onto. After it was extended and enlarged, Justinian built his enormous Nea Christian Church.

THE ALL IMPORTANT CALCULATION

If the existing southern wall is used as the starting point to figure out the location of the temple, the teen feet.

In order to find the exact southern wall during the time of Herod, we have to subtract the one hundred seventeen feet that Justinian added seven centuries later.

If we move the present southern wall back one hundred and seventeen feet and then measure from that point, the precise location of the temple can be determined.

Herod built a plaza from the original southern wall. It was a six hundred feet square and it butted up to the northern wall of the temple square. The plaza was set in between the Antonia fortress and the temple square. The temple area was also a square six hundred feet on each side. A square just like the mezzanine/plaza. In the middle of the temple, square set back towards the west wall, would have been the location of the Jew's temple itself. Then inside the temple was the Holy of Holies.

It was from this point that God would look out from between the two doors. It was right there.

Without the knowledge that one hundred seven- teen feet had been added onto the Temple Mount in the seventh century by Justinian, the calculation for the location of the Holy of Holies would be close, but not precise.

Now looking from inside the temple known as the Holy of Holies—where once sat the ark of the covenant—and outward two thousand cubits, framed in the doors would be the perimeter of the camp of Israel.

Then a short distance from the edge of the perimeter of the circle, just slightly beyond the camp of Judah, would have been the altar of the red heifer. Nearby was the road upon which taxes and polls were collected. Also close by was the fig tree that was standing alongside the road.[31]

All of these items would have been inside the frame of the doors of the Holy of Holies. God could see out to all these things.

And since he had to view all these sacrifices and activities he would also have had to witness the violent death of his only begotten son, Jesus.

Chapter 14

THE GOLGOTHA MYTH

❧

N ot only is tradition the enemy of truth tradition refuses to
die. Even though the temple and the Holy of Holies clearly
point to the exact location of Christ's crucifixion the gainsayers
will continue to argue for the Garden Tomb and the Church of
the Holy Sepulchre as the authentic locations for Jesus' death
burial and resurrection. But it is all myth.

Again we are deeply indebted to the late Dr. Ernest Martin
and his tremendous research in his book the *Secrets of Golgotha*
for this chapter.

TIME TO EXPLODE THE MYTH

Tax collecting and the toll or census were taken outside the
camp.[32] The venue for these activities would also have been
framed within the doors of the Holy of Holies.

If the center of the camp of Israel was calculated and measured from the point of the Dome of the Rock shrine then the Garden Tomb area would fall inside the circle, and therefore inside the camp.

And just as the Church of the Holy Sepulchre was inside the circle—or camp—it too would be disqualified from being the site of Christ crucifixion

But since it has been shown that the real Temple Mount was over the city of David and not where the Dome of the Rock sits, then the Garden Tomb would fall outside the camp.

Then the argument for the Garden Tomb as the actual site where Jesus died, was buried, and rose again would still be in play. For if the point within the circle of the camp were taken from the south east ridge over the city of David then the Garden tomb location would indeed fall outside the camp.

What other facts remain that could sustain and support the common belief for the Garden Tomb area as the real site of the most sacred event?

In other words, why is the Garden Tomb so vigorously argued and religiously held to as the real and still valid place for the crucifixion of Jesus? Where did the tradition come from in the first place, and what facts support the commonly held notion?

SEEING IS BELIEVING

Let us remember the subjective reality of human perception rests on our physical senses. Sadly, seeing is believing! This is how we all tend to roll. People must see with their physical eyes to believe. The Garden Tomb is a physical place that can be seen.

The Garden Tomb presents the pilgrim with that which is physical and tangible evidence. It is there. It can be touched, and experienced with the human senses. But just because it is there doesn't authenticate it as a true and legitimate historic site. Here is a perfect example of how a physical location can be used in a historic twisted deception.

THE FALSE FLAG OF THE GARDEN OF GETHSEMANE

There are a number of facts in the Bible that people can and do associate commonly with physical locations. For example, the garden of Gethsemane. It is a common destination on any tour route in Jerusalem.

As an aside, Jerusalem has been destroyed many times, and with Simon's removal of Mount Zion and the Roman devastation in the first century, Jerusalem has been totally disfigured.

All bets are off regarding any alleged historical location being authentic. In many respects Jerusalem today can be likened unto a religious Disneyland. Case in point the garden of Gethsemane.

There is a very old grove of trees just immediately east of the Kidron Valley across from the sealed eastern gate of the Temple Mount enclosure. This setting is generally held to be the *actual* garden of Gethsemane. It is the spot—they will tell you—where Jesus often prayed and where he was captured the night he was betrayed by Judas.

The particular grove of olive trees, for sure, looks extremely old. The bark on the trees is very rugged and deep and has the feel of being ancient.

Since the trees look as old as Methuselah, it is not hard to lead the people into believing the trees are at least two thousand years old. They definitely look very old. Seeing is believing right?

The ancient look of the trees makes the explanation entirely plausible. The religious tourists are told that these were the actual trees from the time of Jesus.

Furthermore, because the trees are just across the Kidron Valley from the sealed eastern gate through which Jesus was said to have passed it must be the garden of Gethsemane. The apparent confluence of so many facts can be easily woven into the great legend. Especially when the Bible mentions so many of these historical facts.

It is an easy sell. But the pitch is built on a mountain of falsehoods.

In the writings of Flavius Josephus, it says that at the time of the invasion of Jerusalem by the Roman tenth legion—as well as later by Hadrian in the suppression of the Bar Kokhba revolt—all the trees of the city were cut down. Trees were even cut down a great distance from the city. So devastating was the Roman blighting of the land and so thorough the destruction that nothing was left. There was nothing left in the entire area, and for some distance beyond. Nothing.

Early after the destruction, when people came back to visit the area and were told that there once was a city (Jerusalem) standing in that place, they could not believe it, for nothing of Jerusalem remained.

According to Eleazar, who led the Masada revolt that ended in 73 AD there was nothing left but the Roman fortress Antonia. And what's more, Jesus said it would happen.

"And Jesus said unto them, see ye not all these
things? verily I say unto you, there shall not be

left here one stone upon another, that shall not
be thrown down"

(Matt. 24:2)

The fact is the Romans blighted the whole area. No trees
were left standing.

So then how could the grove of trees be the garden of
Gethsemane where Jesus prayed and where he was captured? The
answer is simple: it can't be. It is not the garden of Gethsemane,
but again the unwary pilgrim is duped because seeing the very
old trees is believing!

But what about the Garden Tomb area? What is there to
see with the eyes which would lend people to hold the belief
that this was the place where Jesus died was buried and rose?
Sometimes weeds are hard to pull out because their roots are
deep. But unless you weed them out they will spoil the entire
garden!

What are the claims used to substantiate the Garden Tomb
area as the site where Jesus was killed and buried? What are the
geographical material facts, and how are they manipulated and
made to legitimize the Garden Tomb as the most holy place?

There are three physical features to the site that lead the
faithful astray: there is a garden, there is a tomb, and there is a
skull rock. The *skull rock* is referred to as Golgotha.

All three of these physical features can seemingly be
molded to fit the biblical narrative. Seemingly, but not actually.
They are used to bend the truth. They sculpt the myth.

The tomb of Jesus was near a garden that had much water,
and it was hewn out of rock. There was a stone that rolled in
front of the tomb to seal it.

Firstly, at the Garden Tomb, one can see a slot in front of a tomb where a stone could have been rolled. So this plays into the false narrative. And because this fits nicely into the biblical description of a rolling stone covering a tomb—just like the old trees in the so called garden of Gethsemane—this makes for good story telling. Here, they say, is tangible physical proof.

The physical evidences, such as the rolling stone in front of the tomb, makes it is easy to sculpt the physical feature so that it fits the bible narrative. But it does not fit.

Still, there are guides and preachers who stand before the tomb to reinforce and remind the pilgrim of these obvious features, which they allege are the actual representations of the biblical account.

Remember, we want to know *exactly* where Jesus died because where he died leads to how he died and the full understanding of why he died. There is a huge payoff in this exercise, so stay with me and walk with me to the conclusion. You will be very glad you did.

THE OBSTRUCTION(S)

Here is the first problem with the common story. Remember, to see clearly in the natural sometimes the obstructions need to be removed; the same is true with the mind's eye.

When Jesus died, standing next to him was a Roman centurion.[33] At the moment when Christ gave up his spirit there was a massive earthquake. The earthquake shook the temple. The effect of the earthquake was so powerful that it broke the lintel from which hung the eighty-foot curtain that covered the entrance into the Holy of Holies.

When the thirty-ton lintel broke, it split the eighty- foot curtain from top to bottom. All the people standing around the crucified Jesus saw the event which tore the curtain hanging in front of the temple.

"Now when the centurion, and they that were
with him, watching Jesus, saw the earthquake,
and those things that were done, they feared
greatly, saying Truly this was the Son of God."
(Matt. 27:54)

If the Garden Tomb area on the north side of town, was over one half mile away from the temple, how was it possible for the Romans soldier to have seen the curtain tear?

The only place this could have been witnessed would have been to east of the temple—and high enough to look down into the temple area.

The north side of town, outside the walls of the city, was too low in altitude. And the Garden Tomb was too far away and could not have been seen from the north side of town. In addition, any line of vision would have been blocked by the wall of the city not to mention the Antonia fortress that would have stood in between blocking any line of sight.

The Garden Tomb area, north of the Damascus gate, would not have allowed for the soldier and the others the vantage point to see the curtain tear. The line of view had to be from the east looking west, and not from the north looking south. Jesus died to the east of the temple.

This one simple fact alone begins to obliterate the religious tradition of the Garden Tomb.

The physical features at the Garden Tomb area cause people, nevertheless, to hold tenaciously to the tradition rather than these important facts. The problem is exacerbated because once a person becomes convinced there is an understandable emotional response to standing in the site. When people wholeheartedly buy into the Garden Tomb as the actual site of Jesus' burial and emotion is allowed to enter into perception, it is "Katy bar the door." Any attempt to tell them otherwise is almost impossible. But there is more that holds the people. And it too is deeply emotional.

The other obstacle, and speck in the eye of the pilgrim, is the Golgotha rock. And it is the basis for the Golgotha myth.

ENTER THE GOLGOTHA MYTH

So what about the skull rock just next to the Garden Tomb? Golgotha in more pristine language is called Calvary. This is the preferred word since it is more beautiful than the word Golgotha.

Just a stone's throw from the alleged tomb of Jesus at the Garden Tomb area is a strange rock formation which appears to look like a skull. It sits right behind a Muslim bus station. This strange anomaly is pointed to as the very Golgotha of the bible, hence Calvary.

HE WHO HAS WISDOM WILL KNOW.

When Jews would come into the environs of Jerusalem, they would travel on the road that was east of the city and would pass through a section that separated the northern half of the Mount of Olives from the south- ern half. This was the very same road Jesus traveled when he made the triumphal entry on the donkey.

As the people traveled the road, they would pass by Bethphage which would have been to their right, and just up ahead would have been the fig tree that Jesus cursed. The people came from the east for the most part.

There on that road, just before the camp of Israel, were those who collected taxes from the people. Taxes, as has already been discussed, had to be collected *outside* the camp.[34]

The reason the venue had to be outside the camp was because had any individual come to the area sickly or infirm they would not be allowed inside the camp. But of course they were still required to pay taxes. In order to collect taxes even from the sick it had to be done outside the camp lest the sick person defile and infect the camp. Taxes had to be collected, and it was for this reason the tax collector had to do this outside the camp.

But there was another reason for having such a location outside the camp: the taking of the census or a poll. Again, even the sick had to be counted.

The taking of the census was called the golgolet [Hebrew for *counting of heads*]. And the place of the counting was called the golgolet.

Look at this most amazing scripture.

> "Take ye the sum [in Hebrew rosh meaning census] of all the congregation of the children of Israel, after their families, by the house of their fathers, with the number of their [given] names, every male by their polls"
>
> **(Num. 1:2)**

While the words rosh and *golgolet* are similar, rosh means census, and golgolet means head.

In this sense the meaning is very obvious: the *counting of heads*. Today the place where we vote is called a polling station. It is the place of the golgolet or the counting of heads.

But the term golgolet also had a secondary meaning. It can also mean skull. But the majority of biblical texts suggests it is to be translated as head. And in this it is very clear (as evidenced from the scripture above out of Numbers) that you do not count dead bodies (skulls), instead you count the heads of the living.

So in the taking up of taxes (east of the city on the road into town, and outside the camp) it was a poll tax, or a head tax. The place of the poll tax became known as Golgotha; an obvious derivative of the word golgolet.

Thus the place of the counting of heads became known as Golgotha. Pay you poll tax at Golgotha. The place of the counting of heads.

Jesus was killed at Golgotha, which was outside the camp and east of the temple. The skull rock next to the Garden Tomb and behind the bus depot is a geo- logical anomaly, conveniently used, and inadvertently obscures the real location and meaning of Golgotha.

The real site of Golgotha was on the southern side of the northern portion of the Mount of Olives. The funny looking skull near the Garden Tomb is a subtle physical feature used erroneously to form a false conformity to the biblical narrative.

The Latin word for Golgotha is *Calvary* [from *calvāria*: skull]. The term Calvary is used surreptitiously to make pristine the site of Jesus death, but it was the place of the counting of heads. It is that simple.

When I stop to consider and think of how many songs and hymns have been written and how many sermons preached using the Latin sanitized term Calvary, as a pristine word for Golgotha, there are no words. But the term Calvary invokes an emotional response from religious folk, and that is why it is so important to know the true facts and history. And with its real meaning coming forth and truly explained, it is a sobering and mind boggling consideration.

In so many ways, institutional Christianity is a house of cards built not on the Word but on foolish religious traditions.

Is it any wonder why John (in Revelation[35]) was shocked and astonished when he viewed the Scarlet Woman riding the beast? And can it be any clearer what the meaning of the woman riding the beast clothed in scarlet and drinking the blood of the saints could be? I can relate. It is truly astonishing.

It is high time to really bear down and follow the scripture departing from following foolish notions and traditions.

Chapter 15

WHEN THE FIG TREE PUTS FORTH

৩৵৶

One of the classic biblical prophecies involves fig trees. We covered it in short earlier, but now let us look at it in more detail.

Just a few days before the final moments of Jesus' life, as he rode triumphant into the city on the donkey, he had to pass by the House of Unripe Figs.

He could see the temple and the city several hundred yards ahead. As he approached the city, he wept. He wept because he knew what was going to happen to Jerusalem; he had seen the city, the temple, and all the people in the not too distant future.

As he rode on the beast, he said concerning the city of Jerusalem...

"And when he was come near, he beheld the city, and wept over it, saying, if thou has known, even thou, at least in this thy day, the things which belong unto thy peace! but now they are hid from thine eyes. For the days shall come upon thee, that thine enemies shall cast a trench about thee, and compass thee round, and keep thee in on every side, and shall lay thee even with the ground, and thy children within thee; and they shall not leave in thee one stone upon another; because thou knewest not the time of thy visitation."

(Luke 19:41–44)

He reinforced this statement several days later when he was confronted by his followers.

The disciples who were from the upper region of Galilee had never beheld such a magnificent city as Jerusalem. They were marveling at the grandeur of the city and the glorious temple that Herod had built up and refurbished.

Jerusalem in the first century was more like a Roman city with remarkable and notable buildings. There was a many-storied theatre, an arena for sporting events, several palaces which were the residences for Herod, and many beautiful homes for rich Jews. Then there was the fabulous house of Caiaphas—and don't forget the magnificent golden temple of the Jews. It was altogether a great spectacular city

Herod, while professing to be a Jew, was actually an Edomite, but in reality was subject to Rome. He patterned Jerusalem after Rome. It was a fabulous city, and the simple fishermen from Galilee were over- whelmed by the magnificence and grandeur of what their eyes were feasting upon.

As the disciples were commenting about the temple and how it was adorned with beautiful stones and votive gifts when Jesus broke into their conversation.

"As for these things which ye behold, the days will come, in the which there shall not be left one stone upon another, that shall not be thrown down"

(Luke 21:6)

And indeed the invasion by Rome that would obliterate the city and the temple was a mere forty years in the future. The men were of course astonished. How could this possibly be? They asked Jesus when this would occur, and he gave them a sense for what was to come and then slipped into parable.

"Behold the fig tree, and all the trees; when they now shoot forth, ye see and know of your own selves that summer is now nigh at hand. So likewise ye, when ye see these things come to pass, know ye that the kingdom of God is nigh at hand"

(Luke 21:29–31)

Why didn't he just say all the trees and begin the parable without focusing on the fig tree first? Why did he begin the parable with the focus on the fig tree?

The fig tree was a clear reference to something more than just denoting the time of year when all the trees put forth their leaves. *Behold the fig tree...*

Alluding to the fig tree had something to do with the nearness of the kingdom of God. There was a clear connection.

Just as all the trees putting forth leaves signal the changing of the seasons—in this case the coming of summer—the fig tree would stand out as a sign of the coming of the kingdom of God. When you see the fig tree put forth its leaves meant to look for the fig tree as a sign of the coming kingdom.

Remember that they asked him three questions. When will these things be? The sign of your coming? And the end of the age?

All three questions were answered in the parable. But most specifically he said, summer is now nigh at hand. That meant to these guys that the kingdom was soon. It was coming. He clearly associated the coming kingdom with the fig tree.

What did he mean by *nigh at hand*? Forty years from that moment everything would have been obliterated by the Roman destruction and most of them would be dead.

If he had meant two thousand years in the future, when the Jews returned into the land—as they did in 1948—his answer would have disingenuous and insensitive. That was not his style. He was not just toying with them.

He said the kingdom is near when you see the sign of the fig tree. Two thousand years into the future was not near. Neither would forty years in the future have been fair to his faithful followers.

Consider if you were one of those who was hearing these words. What would your expectation have been? What did they think when he spoke this parable? It was a riddle no doubt, but was Jesus purposely being vague? If they pressed him would he have said, "Well you guys, I wasn't really serious about this coming of my kingdom being soon as mortals count time. Actually it is not until I return one day in the distant future. Maybe two thousand years from now, or so! Sorry guys!"

Really, Jesus?

Jesus wept when he saw the city because he knew what was coming down. He wept because he cared about the loss of life the utter destruction and the bewilderment that would ensue. He knew there would be massive deaths and utter destruction. He cared deeply and especially about these men.

He loved them and would not have lead them on concerning their question. After all, he felt their love and devotion to him and would not have ignored what they had asked.

He told them straight up that the kingdom was near and specifically to look for the nearness indicated in the sign of the fig tree. He told them to look for the sign of the kingdom in the fig tree.

The modern teachers of our day say that this parable was about the prophecy in Isaiah where it is written

> "And it shall come to pass in that day, that the Lord shall set his hand again the second time to recover the remnant of his people, which shall be left, from Assyria, and from Egypt, and from Pathros, and from Cush, and from Elam, and from Shinar, and from Hamath, and from the islands of the sea"

> **(Isa 11:11)**

They see the nation of Israel having been reestablished in 1948—in fact the Jew began to return even before 1948—as the budding of the fig tree. Then there was the war in 1967 that was a miraculous victory for Israel over her Arab neighbors when Jerusalem was recaptured; more evidence of the fig tree. Then, of course, the Yom Kipper war in 1973 when the Golan heights was captured. This again was more signs as the fig tree putting forth its leaves and so, therefore, summer is near. "The kingdom of God is near," they say, "look at Israel which is the fig tree."

There is no doubt that these events coincide with other prophetic scriptures, in fact, with *many* of them, and Israel as we have mentioned is associated no doubt with the fig tree.

But these monumental events were way into the future from the time of the first century when Jesus had uttered the prophecy.

Surely it would be out of his character of love and deep concern for his men to couch the meaning of his words.

Remember, he told them to look to the fig tree as a sign that the kingdom was nigh at hand. Not two thousand years away when Israel returns from its long estrangement from her land but *near*.

The kingdom of God does not come by external observations. The kingdom is now. It is at hand. It is an invisible kingdom. Jesus was telling his loyal followers it is near.

When the fig tree puts forth its leaves, summer is near not far! Keep your eye on the fig tree.

And while there is validity to a second fulfillment in the recent return of the Jews from being without their land, why would he characterize that, in the first century, as near?

It was because he was referring to an invisible inner kingdom. And that access to the inner kingdom would come shortly. *Know ye that the kingdom of God is nigh at hand.*

Those that hold to a future fulfillment concerning the fig tree putting forth its leaves in the far off future are referring to an outward manifestation of God's kingdom which would denote the end of the age.

So then, what more are we to make of this fig tree?

Chapter 16

THEY ALL FLED

৯৯৯

It was the time of the Passover festival. Three times a year, Jews from all over Israel were required to appear before the temple in Jerusalem to give homage and thanksgiving to God. The Passover was the most important of the three convocations. Jews from all over the land would take the road from Jericho and enter the environs of the camp though the eastern gate.

> "Wherefore Jesus also, that he might sanctify the people with his own blood, suffered without the gate. Let us go forth therefore unto him without the camp, bearing his reproach"
> **(Heb. 13:12–13)**

This reference was used earlier to denote the camp. But now in this context, the focus is on the gate. He suffered outside the gate. Which gate? It was called the eastern gate.

The eastern gate was not a gate as one would commonly think. It was different than the eastern gate into the temple square. The gate into the temple was an actual literal gate as we understand the term. The gate into the camp of Israel was more like an entrance way. It was at a place on the roadway that crossed over the line of circumference of the circle into the camp.

In the state of Oregon, there is a narrow pass at the top of Mount Ashland that enters into the state of Oregon. It is a gate into the state. In like manner was the gate into the environs of Jerusalem. All who were coming into Jerusalem would pass through the gate. Jesus passed through this figurative gate when he rode the donkey into Jerusalem. The eastern gate into the temple, by way of contrast, was a literal gate.

It should be clear that the gate outside of which he suffered was the eastern gate located at the very edge of the circumference of the camp, the gate that stood at the border of the camp.

The city was filling up, and Jerusalem would be engorged with people as Israelites from all over the land made the final leg of the journey into the city to keep the important celebration.

They would walk the well-traveled road past Bethphage and Bethany. They would also pass by the altar of the red heifer and the place of the counting of heads where the poll tax was collected.

The road to the temple and the city, which lay to the west, was through the pass between the two sections of the Mount of Olives.

As the day turned toward the evening, he summoned his twelve disciples to a place where they would partake of the Passover meal. The meal was to call to mind the days of servitude in Egypt and the mighty hand of God who brought them out delivering them from bondage.

The Passover meal was instituted thirteen hundred years prior and dated to the time of Moses. Moses had confronted the pharaoh, King of Egypt, and warned him that ten plagues would come upon the land if he did not let God's people leave Egypt. The ten plagues were ordered by God as a means of weakening the strong hand the Egyptians held on the Hebrews.

The last of the ten plagues was to be the most severe. Unless the pharaoh let the people go, every house in the land would be visited with the plague of death on the first born.

The only means of escaping the decree of death was to paint the lintel and door posts of each house with the blood from a sacrificed and unblemished spot- less lamb.

The Jews complied whereas the Egyptian did not. Once the blood was painted on the door, there was a passing over, and that house was not visited with death. Hence the Passover festival was inaugurated to memorialize the supernatural intervention when God passed over and delivered his people from death—and from four hundred years of servitude. The historic night was never to be forgotten.

All Israel was required to make the trek to keep the Passover. It did not matter how far they had to travel; they were required to come and partake of the joyous festival.

Each family was also to bring with them a spotless lamb. It was to be sacrificed at the temple and roasted with fire. Afterward they were to eat the roasted lamb in its entirety; and before sundown.

The slaughter of the lambs commenced at sundown and continued to sundown of the following day. In the early morning around the third hour of the day— there were thousands of lambs that had to be slain—it recommenced from the night before.

It was a perpetual, yearly reminder of the lamb that was slain for them in Egypt and preceded their deliverance from the land of bondage. In addition, they were to make for themselves unleavened bread as part of the meal. For that reason, the Passover was also called the feast of the unleavened bread. It was the bread made in haste.

They had to be ready to leave immediately, so leaven was not used and bread could be quickly baked. In addition, they were to be fully dressed with their sandals on their feet ready to leave promptly. The Hebrews had to be prepared so they could depart Egypt at a moment's notice.

This was a night never to be forgotten. And now the city of Jerusalem was swelling to overflowing with Jews from all over the land, as it was every year. This was the setting for the ensuing events.

Jesus gathered his men to faithfully keep the Passover, but this gathering would be altered and subsequently become known as the Last Supper.

As they all reclined at the table to keep the feast, Jesus became troubled in spirit. It was because he knew the script. One of them would betray him. By now we should all know the story. It would be Judas of Iscariot.

By this time Judas had already become mentally destabilized. His growing doubts about Jesus led him to look for strategic moment in which to betray him into the hands of the priests and elders. Judas had already taken the money they offered—thirty pieces of silver was the agreed upon price—and sold out Jesus choosing Mammon as his god. It was the purchase price for a female slave. But he found the perfect moment he was looking for at the Passover table.

It was there at the Passover table that something monumental and earth shaking was about to take place. This was the straw that broke the camel's back. This was the moment where Judas completely lost it, and broke.

The Jewish Passover feast had been inaugurated and established for hundreds of years in a very specific way; however, it was about to be changed, and changed radically.

In all the proceeding centuries, the night and the meal was to be remembered was by asking four questions. The ritual aspect of the feast was to unfold in a very specific way.

When each question was answered it was followed by the drinking of wine. It was after the first question when Jesus identified the man who would betray him.

This was the answer to the traditional first question.[36]

On all nights we need not dip even once, on this night we do so twice. The salt water into which we dip the *karpas* [potato, onion, or other vegetable] represents the tears we cried while in Egypt.

Similarly, the *charoset* [fruit–nut paste] into which the bitter herbs are dipped reminds us of the cement we used to create the bricks

On all nights we eat the chametz or matzoh, and on this night only matzoh. Slavery: matzoh was the bread of slaves and poor. It was cheap to produce and easy to make. Freedom: matzoh also commemorates the fact that the bread did not have enough time to rise when the Jews hastily left Egypt.

Jesus at this point identified the betrayer.

> "He it is, to whom I shall give a sop, when I have dipped it. And when he had dipped the sop, he gave it to Judas Iscariot, the son of Simon"
>
> **(John 13:26)**

When Judas dipped the sop it was into the bowl of salt water. The salt water represented the tears of the people who long suffered in the land of Egypt.

It was a special symbolic moment as though there was an identification and remembrance of the long years of suffering. Dipping the sop was an identification and participation with suffering.

The most intimate of experiences is the participation and sharing with the hardship of another person's sorrows and sufferings. In our own experience with God, Jesus calls us to enter and share in his suffering. We are directed to go outside the gate and the camp where he suffered and died. He was a man of sorrow acquainted with grief.

Most people want all the goodies though few accept the invitation to share in his sufferings. Outside the camp is where it was patently visualized. Outside the gate and outside the camp mean leaving religious conformity. It means leaving religious tradition.

God entered into the sorrow with his people in Egypt because he was touched by the harsh difficulty of their cruel bondage. He thus brought them out.

Judas was disingenuous and pretentious as he dipped the sop in the bowl of tears. He was a traitor and betrayer. He feigned his sincerity as he did his allegiance to Christ. The worst of transgressors. This is why his name lives in infamy.

But as they continued eating the Passover meal, Christ began to substitute himself in replacement for the traditional elements. Imagine the centuries-old tradition about to be changed. This is what struck Judas right between the eyes. Now was the time to make his move.

The priests and elders of Israel had already deter- mined that Jesus should be killed, but altering and changing the sacred tradition of Passover? This was enough for Judas. Now he was fully convinced that Jesus was to be turned over to the religious authorities. Imagine their religious indignation to centuries- old traditions being altered and changed.

Consider the same reaction today in the Christian world if Jesus was not actually killed on a Roman cross. What outrage! Who is ready and prepared to go outside the camp?

The Jews, though, did not want to kill him during the Passover. After all, it was a joyous celebration. They preferred to kill him after the seven-day festival. Why create a riot?

But the supplanting and changing of the Passover tradition and its literal elements to the body and blood of Christ was far too repugnant and shocking for them. They could no longer hold back their fury. They had come to the tipping point. The kindling temperature had been reached, and there was no stopping them from creating a scene at the Passover.

It would be easier to kill the man than to face the truth of the lackluster emptiness of a long standing traditions.

"For laying aside the commandment of God, ye hold the tradition of men, as the washing of pots and cups: and many other such like things ye do. And he said unto them, Full well ye

reject the commandment of God, that ye may
keep your own tradition"

(Mark 7:8–9)

Tradition is the enemy of truth. But the tradition of the
Passover was based upon the law of Moses, so who could argue?

"In the fourteenth day of the first month
at even is the Lord's Passover. And on the
fifteenth day of the same month is the feast of
unleavened bread unto the Lord: seven days
ye must eat unleavened bread. In the first day
ye shall have a holy convocation: ye shall do
no servile work therein. But ye shall offer an
offering made by fire unto the Lord seven
days: in the seventh day is a holy convocation:
ye shall do no servile work therein."

(Lev. 23:5–8)

But Jesus, several days earlier, had cursed the fig tree. He
was making an enormous statement. It was a statement which
would stand throughout time, but it was not to be understood by
the priests and elders.

When he cursed the fig tree—which represented the Tree
of Knowledge of Good and Evil and hence the law—it was
intended to be remembered through- out the ages. The fig tree
representing the law could not produce the fruit of righteousness.
The law was a curse.

The action of cursing the fig tree was a profound sign
of the ending of the law. The cursing of the fig tree was the
announcement of a change. What had been established by the

law was to be no more. A new covenant would supersede the old.[37]

Even the though the law was holy and righteous it could not, in and of itself, produce holiness or righteousness, and neither could the Passover festival. As a result, Jesus used the fig tree as a message wrapped in a metaphor. He cursed the fig tree.

The elders and priests could not hold back. They moved ahead and put at risk the Passover festival. They sent a throng to arrest him. Armed with clubs and swords, they caught up with them at the garden of Gethsemane.

The priest and elders did not attend the mob scene. They themselves preferring to keep their righteous robes clean. In order to identify Jesus as the culprit, Judas kissed him and thus pointed him out to the soldiers. Now the Roman soldiers knew who to arrest. And they did.

"And from the days of John the Baptist until
now the kingdom of heaven suffereth violence,
and the violent take it by force"
(Matt. 11:12)

They took him to the west side of town and delivered him unto the high priest of the Sanhedrin. The residence of the high priest was on the western hill just outside and west of the temple.

It is fair to say that, even though the religious priests and elders did not have ears to hear nor eyes to see and understand the visual message of the fig tree, neither did the disciples because, when push came to shove, they all fled away in fear. All of them.

Both the deeply rooted fig tree and the mountain representing the kingdom of the Jews that was to flee away at their command, still had its vice like grip on them as well.

In fear they all fled!

Chapter 17

THE MINDSET OF MADNESS

ၥၷ

J udas left the table and went out to the Sanhedrin to inform them as to where to find Jesus and ambush him. It was to be at the garden of Gethsemane.

When he was finally arrested later that night, Jesus was taken to the west side of the city to the house of Caiaphas the high priest.

The high priest Caiaphas had two residences. One was inside the temple square just to the south of the temple, next to the House of Hewn Stones—the other priests also congregated at the House of Hewn Stones when important decisions were to be made. And the other was a residence west of the temple area outside the walls that surrounded the temple.

This house was on the western hill, and it was connected by a courtyard that adjoined with the residence of Annas who was also a High Priest. In the event that something happened to Caiaphas the head High Priest, they were prepared with a backup. Such was the role of Annas.

It was to this house outside the temple area that Jesus was delivered—handed over to be dealt with by the Jewish authorities.

When Peter followed after Jesus, he also came to this house. It was here where he warmed himself by a fire in the courtyard. It was also at this place where he would suffer shame and remorse when he denied that he ever knew the man.

Peter had earlier boasted to the Lord that he would go to prison and even die for him. Jesus replied,

> "Verily I say unto thee, that this day, even in
> this night, before the cock crow twice, thou
> shalt deny me thrice"
>
> **(Mark 14:30)**

It was in the courtyard of this house where the sad moment took place. What guilt he must have suffered.

But we are looking to focus on the mental land- scape of the religious Jews and not the disciple's state of mind.

For several *years* prior to the events of that night, the religious Jews were building a case against Jesus. Their animosity had been growing, and it finally had boiled over. When he was brought to the house of Caiaphas, Jesus was subjected to an intense scrutinizing interrogation by the priests. Now they would get to the truth. It began at midnight.

During the ensuing six hours of examination, which stretched into the early morning, their suspicions and animosity did not abate. On the contrary, their con- tempt only grew to a volcanic level of intolerance. In their religious frenzy, they had made up their mind. Their conviction was well founded, or so it seemed, but the truth was that they were blinded by emotion.

At six in the morning they escorted Jesus to the temple where they met with the other priests at the House of Hewn Stones.

In the temple area, the arrangement of the Holy of Holies—the inner sanctum of the temple—was situated so that it faced eastward. This was arranged so that God's presence, formerly represented by the ark of the covenant with its mercy seat covering the ark, could observe all the sacrifices and decisions that were to be made by the priests. Everything had to be done in the face of God[38] or from the point of view of God.

Both the altar of incense and the altar of burnt offerings were located just a few steps east of the Holy of Holies. God would be watching all these activities.

Two thousand cubits east [little more than half mile] from the Holy of Holies, was another altar. It was also a part of the temple. But it was outside the camp: the altar of the red heifer. All judicial decisions and sacrifices had to be done in the presence of God who faced east from the temple. And even though the altar of the red heifer was over half a mile away, it was still part of the temple.

But when it came to judging Jesus, they had already made up their minds at the house of Caiaphas. They found him guilty of blasphemy, sedition, sorcery, drunkenness, and whore mongering. In their demented minds, he was guilty of all these charges and was deserving of death.

Nevertheless, at sun up, they had to bring him into the temple in front of the face of God to make it official, so that God could see from inside the Holy of Holies what was transpiring.

It would have been breaking of their law not to formally charge him before the face of God.

These men were fanatical when it came to the law. Far be it from them to miss one jot or tittle.

But they had a problem. They were not authorized to execute him, for the authority to bring about capital punishment was vested solely in the hands of the Romans. When it came to capital punishment, the Jews had to yield to the Roman authority.

Since they had made up their minds and voiced their decision as to his guilt the night before at the house of Caiaphas, it was only a formality to officially charge him in the temple. This they did along with the other members of the Sanhedrin. The official action did not take long because they had already made up their minds.

But in order to deal with him in such a way that he could be crucified, they had to take him to Pontius Pilate who *alone* had the authority to kill him.

They marched him across the colonnades that stretched across the plaza between the temple square and delivered him unto Pilate.

"Pilate then went out unto them, and said, What accusation bring ye against this man?

They answered and said unto him, if he were not a malefactor [by our laws], we would not have delivered him up unto thee.

Then said Pilate unto them, take ye him, and judge him *according to your law.*

The Jews therefore said unto him, it is not lawful for us to put any man to death"

(John 18:29–31 emphasis my own)

Now it was the Romans who would examine Jesus. During the course of the Roman interrogation,

Pilate became nervous, for he considered the possibility that Jesus was who he was claiming to be. Pilate grew disquieted and fearful.

When he found that Jesus was from the Galilee region, he was glad to defer, hoping someone other then himself would do the sentencing. So Pilate sent him to Herod (note this was *not* Herod the Great but rather Herod Antipas) who happened to be in town. Herod had the authority to judge those from the region of Galilee. But Herod, after dealing harshly with Jesus, sent him back to Pilate.

On further examination Pontius Pilate grew even more fearful. He could not find fault that warranted the death penalty.

Pilate marched Jesus—who now had a crown of thorns on his head as well as a beautiful purple robe over his shoulders—to the southern wall of the Antonia fortress. The wall overlooked the plaza below where a multitude of Jews along with the elders (the

Sanhedrin) had gathered.

It was on the wall that Pilate became very concerned a riot might break out, for the elders had stirred up the crowd.

"Pilate saith unto them, What shall I do then with Jesus which is called Christ?

They all say unto him, let him be crucified.

And the governor said, Why, what evil hath he done?

But they cried out the more, saying, let him be crucified.

> When Pilate saw that he could prevail
> nothing, but that rather a tumult was made, he
> took water, and washed his hands before the
> multitude, saying, I am innocent of the blood
> of this just person: see ye to it"
>
> **(Matthew 27:22–24)**

And so Pilate delivered Jesus back into the hands of the Sanhedrin so that he might be judged according to their law, i.e. Jewish Law as laid out in Deuteronomy.[39]

He was effectively granting the Sanhedrin leave to deal with Jesus entirely as they saw fit, allowing them to execute Jesus by Pilate's authority but by *their own law*.

This is a critical distinction that is often lost.

Chapter 18

WE HAVE A LAW

ৼৄৎ

P ilate could find no legal basis on which to crucify Jesus. The reason presented was arrived upon at the house of Caiaphas the night before and sprung entirely from Jewish law.

> "Pilate saith unto them, take ye him, and crucify him: for I find no fault in him.
> The Jews answered him, we have a law, and by our law he ought to die, because he made himself the Son of God"
>
> **(John 19:6–7)**

It is a real possibility that the fig tree Jesus had cursed a few days before may have played into their deliberations. How could a man cause a tree to wither save by sorcery? How else would they have interpreted the strange supernatural phenomena?

We have a law...

That was all they could consider. The sound and the words should ring, reverberate, and echo down through the centuries.

We have a law...

It is so important that the world understands this statement. This was the pivotal moment of truth. Jesus the Son of God was to be judged and dealt with according to this law.

It is not just a theological consideration it was and is a spiritual reality.

The mission of redemption lived out by Jesus was planned before man even appeared on earth. The sin of Lucifer had to be dealt with by a predetermined plan.

> "Who verily was foreordained before the foundation of the world, but was manifest in these last times for you"
>
> **(1 Peter 1:20)**

The part Jesus was to play was written into the script before the foundation of the world was set in place. A reasonable way to relate to the notion of a predetermined plan is with the earthly process of movie making. It is a good example as a metaphor of how the physical world works.

A movie is seen on a screen. But before it is visual, it exists as a script. Someone has to write the movie first. It is written as a script. Then, afterwards, it plays out on the big screen. Before it is produced it is written.

You do not see the script. You just see the images and the story unfolding on a screen. The production of a movie is a terrific metaphor.

First things are written in the spiritual realm (the script), and what is written plays out afterwards in the earth realm (the movie on the screen). There are many scriptures that support this reality. Here are but a few.

"According as he hath chosen us in him before the foundation of the world, that we should be holy and without blame before him in love"

(Eph. 1:4)

"For whom he did foreknow, he also did predestinate to be conformed to the image of his Son, that he might be the firstborn among many brethren"

(Rom. 8:29)

Here of course is the a classic one.

"But we speak the wisdom of God in a mystery, even the hidden wisdom, which God ordained before the world unto our glory"

(1 Cor. 2:7)

Lucifer, the antagonist in the story, is a real adversary. It is not a fictional story, and he is not a fictional character. He defected from God and was cast out of the heavenly realms. He was cast down into this world and has power and authority.

Lucifer was given authority to wreak havoc on mankind. And so he does. Just look around. It is more apparent today than ever.

When men break the law of the universe, it is a transgression. Breaking the law is the committing of sin. We are all law breakers. The law requires perfection. Impossible! Yes, keeping the law is impossible. That is why, without forgiveness of sin, there is no a remedy to satisfy the demands of the law. It condemns all. We are all born under the fig tree. We are all born into an untenable situation. We are all born under the law. How do we get out from being under the law?

The solution to the problem began first and had to be solved in the spiritual dimension. The problem of condemnation by the law had to be dealt with and rectified in a preordained way. Since the law condemns all, it had to be removed and taken out of the way. The solution to the problem had to be set up before it could come to the earthly realm. Someone had to break the curse of this problem. This was all taken care of in the script.

It was so designed and written in the spiritual realms that, by keeping the law perfectly and fulfilling the law, there could come a resolution. Yes, but for one problem.

A person would have to live a perfect life on the earth. He would have to live a life that was in accordance with the very law that condemns all. If then that person lived such a life and was judged by the very law he fulfilled and did not break it, this would annul the power of the law. The law that judges everyone. If he were illegally killed, it would fulfill the requirement of the law. Thus the law would be taken out of the way. This is why there is no other name under heaven whereby we can be saved other then Jesus. This is why there is only one way.

Jesus who never sinned against the law, had to be killed by the law—a law that he never broke.

In this way Satan, in killing Jesus at the hands of evil men, overstepped his authority and thus destroyed his authority and the power of the law. Death could not be inflicted when there was/is no breaking of the law. Hence, Jesus rose from the dead.

Satan has authority, when the law is broken, to inflict death, disease, devastation and destruction. He is the god of this world, and a very real adversary. But Satan had Jesus killed *illegally*.

> "Then came Jesus forth, wearing the crown of thorns, and the purple robe.
>
> And Pilate saith unto them, Behold the man! When the chief priests therefore and officers saw him, they cried out, saying, crucify him, crucify him.
>
> Pilate saith unto them, take ye him, and crucify him: for I find no fault in him.
>
> The Jews answered him, we have a law, and by our law he ought to die, because he made himself the Son of God"
>
> **(John 19:5–7)**

But what were the specifics of the law being thus referred to?

Chapter 19

WHAT FEW PEOPLE KNOW

ഇൻ

Here is what few people know, and it is written in the book of Deuteronomy. This was the law the Jewish priests were referring to.

"If a man has a stubborn and rebellious son, which will not obey the voice of his father, or the voice of his mother, and that, when they have chastened him, will not hearken unto them: then shall his father and his mother lay hold on him, and bring him out unto the elders of his city, and unto the gate of his place; and they shall say unto the elders of his city, this our son is stubborn and rebellious, he will not obey our voice; he is a glutton, and a drunkard. And all the men of his city shall stone him with stones, that he dies: so shalt thou put evil away from among you; and all Israel shall hear, and fear.

And if a man has committed a sin worthy of death, and he be put to death, and thou hang him on a tree: his body shall not remain all night upon the tree, but thou shalt in any wise bury him that day; (for he that is hanged is accursed of God;) that thy land be not defiled, which the Lord thy God giveth thee for an inheritance."

(Deut. 21:18–23)

The specific law that was being referred to was this law in Deuteronomy. According to this law and how they applied the law, Jesus must die. Jesus was the rebellious son, and according to the law of the Jews this meant there was to be a stoning. And for one who committed capital offense it was crucifixion on a tree.

When they took Jesus out of the temple area through the eastern gate also called the Miphkad gate (gate of the red heifer or altar of burnt ashes) he was carrying his crosspiece. Many think he was carrying a Roman cross, which today is, of course, the very symbol and branding of Christianity, but it was only the crosspiece called in Latin a *patibulum*.

Remember, Jesus had to be executed according to Jewish law not Roman law. While Jesus was taken to the Roman authority, he was eventually dealt with according to the Jewish law. Even then the piece of wood (the patibulum or crosspiece) was too heavy and they summoned Simon of Cyrene to carry it for him. They went eastward towards the Mount of Olives.

The sacrifice of God's only son had to be from the point of view from the doorway of the Holy of Holies so that, from God's point of view looking east, God could witness the perfect sacrifice of his son, Jesus.

But as mentioned, there was actually a third place where the Sanhedrin met, and that was at the House of Unripe Figs.

While it is not mentioned in the New Testament biblical record *per se*, it was a matter of Jewish proto- col and law that determinations for ultimate decisions for issues outside the camp be made at the House of Unripe Figs. The Sanhedrin had gathered there to make the specific and official decision for the sentencing of Jesus.

When they gathered in the early morning hour of six at the Chamber of Hewn Stones, it was a foregone conclusion. He was guilty of numerous crimes, and it took little time to go through the formality.

Now that Pilate had handing him back over to the Jews, so also was the case of his sentencing when the priest assembled outside the camp at the House of Unripe Figs.

According to the law of the Jews he was to be excommunicated (made a non-Jew), stoned to death, and hung on a tree.

This law in Deuteronomy paints a different picture of the crucifixion of Jesus than is commonly known. First, he would be treated as a non-Jew or gentile, second he would be killed by stoning and finally this would occur on a tree of crucifixion.

The fact of him having to be stoned, which is virtually unknown to the Christian world, is even attested to and confirmed by the very writing of the Sanhedrin found in the Babylonian Talmud.

MISHNAH. If then they find him innocent, they discharge him; but if not, he goes forth to be stoned, and a herald precedes him [crying]: so and so, the son of so and so, is going forth to be stoned because he committed such and such an offense, and so and so are his witnesses. Whoever knows anything in his favor, let him come and state it.

GEMARA. Abaye said: it must also be announced: on such and such a day, at such and such an hour, and in such and such a place [the crime was committed], in case there are some who know [to the contrary], so that they can come forward and prove the wit- nesses zomemim. And a herald precedes him etc. This implies, only immediately before [the execution], but not previous thereto. [in contradiction to this] it was taught: on the eve of the Passover Yeshu meaning Jesus, was hanged.[40]

THE LIVING TREE

But what drives the point home and puts an end to any argument to the contrary is made patently clear by the apostle Paul.

In the book of Galatians, the apostle Paul was writing to dispel confusion regarding the law as it pertained to the gospel of grace.

There were Jews who were trying to teach that, in spite of what Jesus had accomplished at his death (the forgiveness of sin), certain Jewish rites must also be kept; such as circumcision etc. These people, which included the apostle Peter, were in effect Judaizing the gospel.

They all met with harsh criticism and rebuke from Paul because they were adding to what was not necessary for salvation. Paul argued that salvation was by grace alone, and in no way could it be earned by the adding of Jewish rites or any of the laws of the Jews.

In his letter to the Galatians he made an astonishing statement, and it is this statement that nails it.

> "Christ hath redeemed us from the curse of the
> law, being made a curse for us: for it is written,
> Cursed is every one that hangeth on a tree"
> **(Gal. 3:13 emphasis my own)**

Did you notice? Most would likely only have followed the argument about grace versus the law and the curse. But there is something in this scripture that tends to be overlooked because the focus is on the apologetic. Yet this one piece of evidence seals the deal on how, why, and where Jesus was executed.

Paul was making a critical point of the fact that it is written into the law of the Jews how a law breaker— such as Jesus who was accused and charged—should be treated. Again, this is what it says in Deuteronomy:

> "If a man has a stubborn and rebellious son,
> which will not obey the voice of his father, or
> the voice of his mother, and that, when they
> have chastened him, will not hearken unto
> them: then shall his father and his mother lay
> hold on him, and bring him out unto the elders
> of his city, and unto the gate of his place;
> and they shall say unto the elders of his city,
> this our son is stub- born and rebellious, he
> will not obey our voice; he is a glutton, and
> a drunkard. And all the men of his city shall

stone him with stones, that he dies: so shalt thou put evil away from among you; and all Israel shall hear, and fear.

And if a man has committed a sin worthy of death, and he be to be put to death, and thou hang him on a tree: his body shall not remain all night upon the tree, but thou shalt in any wise bury him that day; (for he that is hanged is accursed of God;) that thy land be not defiled, which the Lord thy God giveth thee for an inheritance."

(Deut. 21:18–23)

When Paul made the statement about what was written, and referred to in Deuteronomy, he is pointing out that according to the Deuteronomic Code of the Jews themselves everyone who hangs *on a tree* is cursed. He was quoting from the Old Testament law of the Jews and the word for tree in the Hebrew language of Deuteronomy is ets, which in Hebrew means *a living tree*. It is correctly translated from *ets* in Hebrew into the Greek language of the new Testament as the word *xulon* [a living tree].

It is critical to make this point clear as the implications are monumentally significant.

Chapter 20

THE CONSTANTINE EFFECT: CROSS OR TREE?

୨∘୧

So then was it a Roman cross or a tree—or *was* the Roman cross a tree? The two terms are used seemingly interchangeably in all the translations. Why is it that, in some places within the scripture, the word cross is used as the instrument for Christ's crucifixion while, in other places, the word tree is used?

Is it possible there is a major contradiction? What has happened historically? How can this be; or is this even an argument at all? And most of all why should we care?

In various scriptures there are times when the word *cross* is used and there are times when the word *tree* is used. The scriptures jump back and forth between these two words. It is even more confusing from one translation to another translation.

In the Nelson Study Bible for example Acts 5:30 reads:

"The God of our fathers raised up Jesus whom
you murdered by hanging him on a tree"

But the New American Standard Bible presents
Acts 5:30 as:

"The God of our fathers raised up Jesus,
whom you had put to death by hanging Him on a cross."

See the contradiction between the two renderings? Each translation uses a different word. Furthermore, later on in the same New American Standard version in the book of Galatians it says:

"Cursed is everyone who hangs on a tree"
(Gal. 3:13).

So not only are there contradictions between translations as evidenced in the two examples, there is even a contradiction within the same translation. The NASB cannot decide whether to use the word *cross or tree*. The translators had a real problem on their hands. This conundrum, this contradiction, is really important to look into. We must get to the bottom of the perplexing problem. We must get to the root of the matter.

Which is it, cross or tree? Church tradition is sacrosanct on the question: it is cross. Is the distinction even important? Are we straining out a gnat so to speak?

Was Jesus killed on a cross? Could he have been killed on a tree? How was this left to ambiguity? The symbol of the Roman cross is the centuries-old enduring brand of Christianity.

Why does it even matter? Why even consider to try and seek to change it now?

Let's begin to lay an ax to the root and find why this is a most significant matter for consideration.

The world was set up for a colossal misstep during the rise to power of Constantine the Great, the first Christian emperor. His mother, Helena, was the first to assume that Jesus was killed—along with the two thieves—on the Roman cross. Helena, who was frequented by dreams, was reported to have found three crosses at the location where Constantine would later order the building of the Church of the Holy Sepulchre.

The church was to be located on the west side of Jerusalem where a shrine to Zeus had been formerly set up in the second century. The massive elaborate church was to be the replacement for the Jews' former temples. It stands today as a memorial and monument to the man who marked a turning point in the history of Christianity—Constantine the Great.

After his great vision at the Milvian Bridge in 312 AD and his subsequent military victories, he grew in power and renown. It was at the famous bridge where, evidently, he was told to conquer under the sign of the cross, and he did.

His military successes advanced his acclaim and added to his renown and credibility. The many military successes seemed to assume the legitimacy that God was certifying the cross.

Constantine's victories, or so it was believed, were God's affirmation as to Constantine's vision of the cross. And as his renown grew so did the acceptance of the cross, which would become Christianity's enduring symbol and logo. The faith had a brand, and it was the Roman cross.

Constantine finally took over the entire Roman Empire. The momentum of his rise came with intoxicating power and ushered in the pre-eminence of the Roman cross.

The effect of Constantine's emperorship—both the massive church building (the church stands strong after seventeen centuries) and the Council of Nicaea—had monumental impact on the world. One of those rarely known effects was in relationship to the three codices of scripture.

A codex is a manuscript. The term codex is primarily used to denote an ancient manuscript. The oldest codex for the Bible dates, not coincidentally, to the fourth century AD. There were no biblical New Testament manuscripts that date before the fourth century.

The three codices of the fourth century were all written in Greek: The Codex Sinaiticus, Codex Vaticanus, and Codex Vercellensis. But the question is who penned them? It is interesting that the Codex Sinaiticus, the oldest of them, was produced in the middle of the fourth century.

The codex was produced *after* the ascent of Constantine to emperorship and after the Council of Nicaea.[41] The codex, most certainly lay in the shadow of what had become the legal religion of Christianity already branded and coded with the Roman cross.

By the mid-fourth century, the Christian faith had come on full force.

The momentum of the high tide of Christianity—a tidal change from an illegal religion to a legal religion—was more like a tsunami which completely inundated the Roman Empire. The whole sea change was set in motion by the force of the personality of Emperor Constantine.

It is not difficult to imagine how the nature of the massive change would have had significant influence on the scribes of that day. Especially in the development of the handwritten codex of the fourth century. In the mid-fourth century, Christianity was in fashion and full bloom. Seventeen centuries later, the religious brand has remained.

It is time for all to develop a below-the-surface insightful understanding to the scriptures.

It should be remembered that Pontius Pilate placed the sign above the head of Jesus: Iesus Nazarenus Rex Iudaeorum [Jesus of Nazareth, King of the Jews]. It was also written in Hebrew and Greek. Jesus spoke in Aramaic and Hebrew. So words that Jesus spoke in the first century had to be translated into the Greek of the fourth century.

The problem with words is that they can have a life of their own. They often evolve over time and acquire different meanings. New ideas can be attached to words as time goes by, especially over centuries.

Take for example the word *gay*; only forty years ago it meant happy or joyful, but today the primary connotation is homosexual. There are many examples how words attach new meanings over time, and this is just a glaring example. Culture has a powerful influence on language.

What would have happened to words that were subject to three hundred years of linguistic drift from the first century to the fourth century? And what effect would time have on the codex? Especially when those who penned the codex were under the influence and bias of the Greek Orthodox Church.

Take for example the words of Jesus when he said (in Hebrew mind you):

"If any man will come after me, let him deny
himself, and take up his cross daily, and follow
me"

(Luke 9:23)

We must learn to develop a penetrating below- the-surface
vision into the scriptures. This classic scripture has much that
remains hidden because of language. Jesus did not say this in
Greek, where the word *stauros* is used for cross, he said it in
Hebrew. But in all translations of the bible today—from the
fourth-century codex written in Greek—the word for cross was
stauros.

And stauros in the Greek meant something far different
then what Jesus meant. The Greek records Jesus as saying "take
up your cross and follow me."

Millions and millions of people—in fact tens of mil- lions
of people—have searched the internet seeking to find out what
Jesus meant when he said, "take up your cross."

Had they known the exact language Jesus used in the first
century they would have been able to figure it out for themselves.

And now we get into murky waters. There are four
words needed to be analyzed and looked into with spiritually
penetrating eyes: *staroo, stauros, xulon*, and *patibulum*. The first
three are Greek words, and the fourth is Latin.

The word *staroo* in Greek means to crucify. And the word
stauros means spike, or he was staroo-ed, crucified on a stauros,
or a spike. But the modern translations translate the word stauros
as cross. How should it be most properly rendered in the modern
translations, a spike or a cross? The Jehovah's Witnesses say
spike. They are closer to the honest and best interpretation of the
word stauros, but they are wrong objectively.

If it were rendered a spike, there is a problem with the mind picture it conveys. If he were nailed to a spike—a stauros—both his hands would have been lifted up over his head. Then with one hand over the top of the other, one nail would have had to go through both hands. If that were the case—which is more in line with the idea of a spike—how could Pilate have placed a sign over his head saying (in three languages) Jesus of Nazareth, King of the Jews?

In addition, the spike (stauros) would have been a large piece of timber weighing more than either Jesus or Simon of Cyrene could have carried. Jesus was not killed on a spike, yet this is the meaning of the word stauros. But remember the Greek scribes under the influence of Emperor Constantine used the word stauros, but to *them* it meant a cross.

But the word stauros could have been confused and misunderstood three hundred years later by the fourth-century scribes.

The fact of the matter is the word stauros or spike, instead of meaning he was put on a spike, could have easily meant *to be spiked* (e.g. by nails). Especially misunderstood three hundred years later after the actual event of his crucifixion.

And fourth-century scribes would have been hard pressed not to agree with the Roman cross, having been significantly influenced by the power of the Constantine effect.

They would have most assuredly aligned with the Council of Nicaea (officiated by Constantine)—not- withstanding what had become the brand of the faith—and defaulted to cross. And so stauros to them meant cross, a Roman cross.

The influences of the day would have overwhelmingly required a word to convey a specific mind picture. After all it was Constantine who had the vision of the cross at the Milvian

Bridge and whose mother uncovered three Roman crosses. It was the Greek word stauros that was selected for the codex.

All three codices make the same use of the word stauros suggesting a Roman cross. Why? It was because of the fourth-century scribes under the aegis of Constantine and his cross vision and his mother Helena's visions.

Here is an example of where the term cross is used in the Greek language and the word for cross in the translations is the word stauros.

> "And you, being dead in your sins and the uncircumcision of your flesh, hath he quickened together with him, having forgiven you all trespasses; blotting out the handwriting of ordinances that was against us, which was contrary to us, and took it out of the way, nailing it to his cross"
>
> **(Col. 2:14)**

The word for cross used here in the Greek is stauros, but is it stauros? Should the word in all the translations be the word cross?

No! Here is the amazing error.

It is amazing to see how there are verses that use the word stauros throughout all the common translations. These renderings are taken from the fourth-century codex. Again remember, they were all overshadowed by the Constantine effect.

Yet in other scriptures in the New Testament the word *xulon* is used when you would expect the word stauros. Xulon means tree. Why is the scripture not consistent? Why xulon and not stauros? Why the inconsistency?

In the book of Deuteronomy it says:

"His body shall not remain all night upon the tree, but thou shalt in any wise bury him that day"

(Deut. 21:23)

And so does Paul when he quotes the Law in Galatians. Is it *xulon* [tree] or *stauros* [cross]? Since a cross is made from a tree what difference does it make? This distinction is seriously important, but scholars and scribes and teachers shrug it off as not important at all.

Why then didn't Jesus say take up your tree and follow me. That of course, would have been impossible. How can you take up your tree and walk with him daily? This was a real problem for the interpreters and translators.

Jesus was not nailed to a cross or a spike. He was crucified to a patibulum, and then *hung* from a tree. What was a patibulum?

It was the crosspiece not the entire cross as we think of the cross. Yet seen on all the Christian churches is Constantine's Roman cross.

When Jesus said (as it comes down in translations from the codex) "take up your cross," the word stauros is used by Greek scribes, meaning to them the traditional Roman cross. It would be better rendered and understood that what Jesus was saying more rather was take up your patibulum, or at the very least a Hebrew word that was synonymous with patibulum.

Now there is harmony. Jesus was crucified on a patibulum. The patibulum had to be lifted up and attached to a tree according to the law of the Jews as clearly written in Deuteronomy 21, and which was referred to and quoted by Paul in the book of Galatians.

Today, there are attempts to illustrate the idea of the patibulum as it is placed on top of a spike forming a T. The idea is to somehow keep the tradition of stauros and the Christian Pagan Roman cross alive, or to somehow make it consistent with the Greek Tau which or letter T.

But this idea refuses to reconcile with the objective reality.

Paul quoted in Galatians, "cursed is everyone who hangs on a tree." The lines are blurred by making a dead piece of wood—a cross—as though it were a tree. But Jesus was killed according to the law of the Jews.

Again the word in Hebrew for tree is ets, a living tree not a dead piece of wood. I know what you are probably thinking: *who cares*? But stay with me.

And the picture from Deuteronomy was that of being hung from a tree, not nailed to it. As it was a tree—a living tree—there was room on the living tree for Pontius Pilate to place a sign over the head of Jesus that read: "Jesus of Nazareth King of the Jews" in three languages.

When all the scriptures are taken together, they paint a decisively clear but *different* picture than that of which tradition describes.

For the past seventeen centuries, every Christian teacher, scribe and preacher seems to have a mechanism which defaults back to the era of Constantine and cannot cut through the bias of the fourth century to the truth. Constantine and his vision of the pagan Roman cross became the brand.

While the nuances seem minuscule and inconsequential, they are actually enormous. By following through to the outcome at the end of the consideration, there is a Praise God payoff for the rest of your life.

Nonetheless, it was the Constantine effect that covered over the details, preventing the truth from being known. The brand of the pagan cross was firmly in place and the true facts were obscured and lost from sight.

Chapter 21

THE MORNING OF THE CRUCIFIXION

ೂೆ

L et us return to the very day Jesus was crucified and revisit that morning. There are two timelines presented in the scriptures which differ concerning the actual time Jesus was crucified. One account (in Mark 15:25) has Jesus crucified at nine am. another (in John 19:14) at twelve noon.

If the bible is the infallible word of God, how can there be two different timelines? Scholars have tried to offer reasonable explanations for the discrepancy, but none really satisfy. How are we to deal with and reconcile the problem when confronted with the contradiction? The issue presents quite a conundrum!

Remember the codex?

The codices were formed in the mid-fourth century. Over three hundred years had passed from the time of the actual event. The scribes of the fourth century were trying to reassemble the facts. There were only fragments and verbal traditions available in the fourth century to put together the story. Those fragments of information formed the codex.

In order to explain the contradiction, it should be remembered that a few details could have been mistaken in the writing of the codex. But while the letter of the word may have conflict the spirit of the word is a different story. Though the letter of the word may have a small number of contradictions, the spirit of the word is purely infallible and never changes. It is accurate. It is the Word of God.

As already noted, the whole mind picture of the tree as opposed to the cross appears to have had the same problem with the true facts. Nevertheless, it is very important to consider which time is correct. So then, was it nine am., or twelve noon?

When Jesus was led from the house of Caiaphas and Annas it was near six in the morning. We know this because the body of the Sanhedrin met in the temple at that early hour to formally decide and legally make the determination as to his guilt. They had to wait until sun up. Sun up was six am.

And remember, the judgment had to be in front of the Holy of Holies so God would be able to watch what was happening. It had to be before the Lord.

After the determination of his guilt, Jesus was marched out of the temple area over two colonnades, or the plaza area, which was six hundred feet long. He was taken to the Roman Antonia fortress and on to the praetorian where Pontius Pilate awaited him. There at the praetorian, he was interrogated and scrutinized by Pontius Pilate.

How long did this take?

When it was found that he was from Galilee, Pilate turned him over to Herod who was in town. Herod had jurisdiction over the Galilee region and could legally judge what to do with the man. Herod had his residence on the west side of Jerusalem, outside the wall of the Antonia fortress.

How far was it to Herod's place from the praetorian? In escorting Jesus, they would have had to walk at least two hundred yards from the praetorian to the northern gate of the Antonia fortress. Then they turned left and walked to Herod's place another couple hundred yards to his house.

How long would that have taken, and how long was Jesus under scrutiny at Herod's palace?

At Herod's residence they beat him, placed a purple robe on him and a crowned him with thorns. The cohort (five hundred) of soldiers watched. It would have taken time to assemble those men. And they would have been very raucous. The very nature of the mob with the countless hurled insults would have stretched out the time.

But how much time?

Then he was taken back to Pilate again for re-examination. More time transpired. Pilate got scared and took him back to the Jews. Afterward Pilate became even more disturbed. He turned back to the praetorian and examined him again.

How much time did this take?

Finally, he was brought back before the mob of Jews including the priests and Sanhedrin who were standing below the southern wall of the Antonia fortress in the square six-hundred-foot courtyard. Pilate was standing on the wall talking to the people below. Jesus was standing next to him as he was presented to the crowd. They screamed for his crucifixion, and Pilate washed his hands in front of them while he stood above on the wall.

Again how long did this take?

Then Pilate turned him over to the Jews. Jesus was led down from the wall to the courtyard. He was led down from the wall over a number of steps to the courtyard. Then he was led six hundred feet across the courtyard to the temple square. He entered the temple square through one of its northern gates.

There he was burdened with the patibulum (cross- piece) and led out the eastern gate carrying it. He was led over the bridge that spanned the brook Kidron. Soon thereafter, Simon the Cyrene was recruited to help carry the patibulum. It would be over half a mile to arrive outside the camp of Israel. Jesus, by this time, was weakened and would have had to walk slowly.

How much time?

In light of all these events it was unlikely that Mark's time of nine am. works. The nine am. crucifixion was probably too early. They didn't have wrist watches in those days and therefore reckoned time by the position of the sun in the sky. It was most likely an approximation.

But something else of vital importance had to take place during that interim which was not recorded per se in the New Testament scriptures. It is alluded to in Deuteronomy.

The Sanhedrin had to fulfill another duty, and it had to take place at the House of Unripe Figs—again we are deeply indebted again to the late Ernest Martin for his remarkable research in bringing this important fact to light.

In Bethphage, the Sanhedrin were obliged to keep a protocol for dealing with all sorts of issues. The protocol would have to take place outside the camp. The issue facing the Sanhedrin with Jesus was complicated and, in some ways, unprecedented.

In the book of Deuteronomy, in the seventeenth chapter, was the instruction for how they would have go about their business.

"If there be found among you, within any of thy gates which the Lord thy God giveth thee, man or woman, that hath wrought wickedness in the sight of the Lord thy God, in transgressing his covenant, and hath gone and served other gods, and worshiped them, either the sun, or moon, or any of the host of heaven, which I have not commanded; and it be told thee, and thou hast heard of it, and inquired diligently, and, behold, it be true, and the thing certain, that such abomination is wrought in Israel: then shalt thou bring forth that man or that woman, which have committed that wicked thing, unto thy gates, even that man or that woman, and shalt stone them with stones, till they die. At the mouth of two witnesses, or three witnesses, shall he that is worthy of death be put to death; but at the mouth of one witness he shall not be put to death. The hands of the witnesses shall be first upon him to put him to death, and afterward the hands of all the people. So thou shalt put the evil away from among you"

(Deut. 17:2–7)

It was also at Bethphage, in the House of Unripe Figs, where not only death sentences were determined and validated, but also where excommunication of the extremely wicked took place. While Jesus was judged guilty inside the temple environs, he had to be sentenced outside the camp at Bethphage.

They were instructed to take him to the city gate. The gate would have been two thousand cubits due east from the temple. They were to put him to death by the word of at least two witness (they had at least ten witnesses) by stoning, and to purge the evil.

Jesus was considered an elder. He was called rabbi and was formerly allowed to teach in their very temple.[42] In order for them to make a full purge, Jesus had to be discredited.

"If there arise a matter too hard for thee in judgment, between blood and blood, between plea and plea, and between stroke and stroke, being matters of controversy within thy gates: then shalt thou arise, and get thee up into the place which the Lord thy God shall choose; and thou shalt come unto the priests the Levites, and unto the judge that shall be in those days, and inquire; and they shall shew thee the sentence of judgment: and thou shalt do according to the sentence, which they of that place which the Lord shall choose shall shew thee; and thou shalt observe to do according to all that they inform thee: according to the sentence of the law which they shall teach thee, and according to the judgment which they shall tell thee, thou shalt do: thou shalt not decline from the sentence which they shall shew thee, to the right hand, nor to the left. And the man that will do presumptuously, and will not hearken unto the priest that standeth to minister there before the Lord thy God, or unto the judge, even that man shall die: and

thou shalt put away the evil from Israel. And
all the people shall hear, and fear, and do no
more presumptuously"

(Deut. 17:8–13)

At Bethphage, the Sanhedrin excommunicated Jesus. In their eyes he was to be regarded as a gentile. So not only was he stoned on a tree, he was also regarded as a non-Jew and thus barred from ever entering the camp again.

Though he was to die, the message of excommunication had its effect in discrediting the veracity of his ministry.

In order for all these things to transpire, he was most likely executed nearer to twelve noon. So while there is conflict between the two accounts for the actual time of the crucifixion, the spirit of the actual story is real, true, and valid.

Chapter 22

THE ACRIMONY AND THE IRONY

သာက

No doubt the acrimony and slander will begin to fly because the tradition is strong. Emotions are powerful chains, and much feeling has been attached to the "old rugged cross." It means so much to so many. But what has it meant to the Jews? Please keep in mind what was written in the book of Galatians by the great apostle Paul.

> "Christ hath redeemed us from the curse of the law, being made a curse for us: for it is written, cursed is every one that hangeth on a tree"
>
> **(Gal 3:13)**

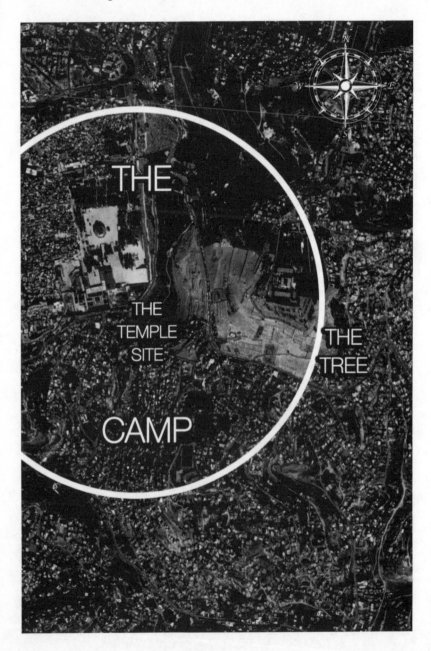

He was hanged on a *xulon* [a tree] not a *stauros* [a cross, a pagan Roman cross]. It is clear it was a living tree (*ets* in Hebrew).

Over the centuries, to the Jews, the use of the Roman cross has come to mean, ironically, a symbol of death, but not the death of Jesus.

It is ironic because Jews do not initially associate the Roman cross with the death of Christ. Instinctively they attribute the cross to pogroms, persecutions, and the murder of their own people. They associate the cross with the persecution and the deaths at the hands of the Church.

When Jews were banned from Jerusalem, it was first by the Romans. Then, afterwards, under the symbol of the Constantine Roman/Pagan cross by the Christians. Yes, the Jews were banned from Jerusalem by the Christians.

Even though later Jerusalem had changed into the hands of the Muslims, Jews were not allowed in, and this was because of the Christians.

Before the Christians took over the city of Jerusalem in the fourth century, the name was change to Aelia Capitolina, and Israel was changed to Palestine. This was done by Rome.

It was the emperor of Rome who banished them from the city after killing over a million Jews. Then came the great Roman emperor Constantine who did the same as his predecessors. In fact, it was Constantine who had the ears of Jews cut off when they were trying to rebuild their temple in the fourth century. When a Jew was thus disfigured, it rendered him unfit to build the temple according to the Jewish law.[43] The Jews associate Christian Rome under Constantine's empire along with the Roman empire under Caesar. They make no distinction.

So, Jews see all Christians and non-Christians as the same. They are all oppressors and gentiles. The Jews make no distinction.

By the seventh century, when Muslims began to take over the city, agreements were made between the bishop of the Church of the Holy Sepulchre and the Muslims that forbade Jews from re-entry into the city.

When Jews were forced to live in other lands, they were forced, under the sign of the Roman cross, to convert or die. During the infamous Spanish Inquisition, Jews fled to other parts of the world looking for safe haven.

When the black plague struck in the middle of the fourteenth century, the Church blamed the Jews for the problem that wiped out half of the population of Europe. It was all done under the sign of the pagan Roman cross.

The great Christopher Columbus (claimed to have been a Jew) led expeditions, as did other explorers, into the new world looking for safe havens for the Jews.

Under Columbus they settled and lived in Jamaica without harassment from the Catholic Church for over one hundred years. But the point is they were forced to flee. It was because of the persecution done under the sign of the Roman cross. Many Jews even changed their names to avoid the terrible trouble inflicted by the Church whose brand was the again the Roman cross.

The Jews fled from the cross and from those who were obliged to enforce the cross, the so called Christians.

Martin Luther hated the Jews, and it was he that significantly helped bring about the Protestant Reformation. He too was a man adhering and holding up the Roman cross. Nonetheless, to the Jew, it meant something entirely different.

During the era Hitler's Third Reich, as Jews were herded like cattle into boxcars for deportation to concentration camps, Catholic priests were sprinkling holy water on the ramparts. They did this while the Roman cross hung from their belts and in plain sight from around their necks.

It should not be a secret as to why a Jewish person cringes when he or she hears someone speaking in a German accent. The history of holocaust where six million Jews were murdered and the last two thou- sand years strewn with the bodies of persecuted Jews is in embedded in the DNA. It is also the case with the Roman cross.

The carnage across the centuries they associate with the pagan Roman cross.

This is what comes to mind when the Jew sees the Roman cross. It is almost as though the cross is what veils their eyes and keeps them from seeing who Jesus really was to them. To the Jew, the Roman cross of Constantine was and is anathema.

But strange as it seems, the bible itself actually teaches nothing about a pagan Roman cross. It has been a massive misstep and imposition coming from all that transpired during the fourth century under the rule of Constantine. The stauros of the Greeks was not the instrument of the death of Jesus Christ.

Let's take a closer look.

The actual nailing of Jesus to the patibulum and the lifting him up had to be accomplished without Jewish hands; in order for them to remain clean for the Passover, it had to be done by the Roman soldiers.

Handling the person of Jesus during the festival would have defiled the priests and made them unfit for the Passover. The Roman soldiers did the dirty work of nailing him to the patibulum, but it was done according to the Jewish law. And according to that law he had to be stoned, as well as crucified.

Stoning was more than the mere execution of a person it was a form of torture.

When Pilate placed the sign over the patibulum which said Jesus of Nazareth, King of the Jews, it was a trigger that instigated violent emotions in those coming into town for the Passover. They began to pick up stones and hurl them at Jesus as he hung there. But according to their law, the casting of the first stones commenced with the priests.

It is not hard to understand their intense displeasure with Jesus. They had not soon forgotten the episode of the woman caught in adultery. The classic event was most certainly etched into the memory of the priests, because after all, he embarrassed them and challenged their authority.

When the woman was about to be stoned to death by the priests, Jesus stepped in to rescue her.

> "he lifted up himself, and said unto them, He
> that is without sin among you, let him first cast
> a stone at her"
>
> **(John 8:7)**

Publicly humiliated at the rebuke, the priests slithered away, but they didn't forget.

Now it was their chance to even the score. Those from the House of Unripe Figs were not tainted by sin and had their pride involved. After all, their judgments were free from the effect of sin. At least according to the what the House of Unripe Figs purported to say. In their own minds, their judgment was sacrosanct.

In the poison of their self-righteousness, they would get their revenge. This time they would cast the first stones. They got their man.

> "If he be the King of Israel, let him now come
> down from the cross, and we will believe him.
> He trusted in God; let him deliver him now, if
> he will have him: for he said, I am the Son of
> God."
>
> **(Matt. 27:42–43)**

The self-righteous priests were reveling in what they mistakenly determined to be Christ's just due. He deserved what was coming. Now who looks the fool? It was the priests who would be the first to cast the stones.

But they couldn't get to close to him. In fact, it was *unlawful* to even come within a few meters of Jesus. It was the law. They had to keep a distance, or they would become defiled and unfit for the Passover celebration.

Jesus was crucified while, half a mile away, multitudes who had gathered for the Passover were having their unblemished Passover lambs slaughtered in the temple.

Here he hung, nailed to a patibulum that had been hoisted and attached to a tree alongside two thieves on the well-traveled road that led into the city and temple.

The crowd that had assemble had no idea they were observing the very fulfillment of the Passover. The very Lamb of God.

Chapter 23

THE TREE

෨ඐ

In order to remain ritually clean, the actual nailing of Jesus to the patibulum and the lifting him up had to be accomplished without Jewish hands. It had to be done by the Roman soldiers because handling the person of Jesus would have defiled the priests and made them unfit. They would have been disqualified from participation in the Passover. Stoning was more convenient because they did not have to touch him.

When Pilate placed his sign on the tree, it set off a violent reaction in the Jews, for it was insulting to those coming into town. They picked up stones and hurled them at Jesus as he hung there. What a horrible thing to have been one of those who had thrown a stone.

But there was something very unusual that happened, or rather did *not* happen at that moment. In fact, it was something so remarkable and so astonishing it is beyond belief. Those that stood by and those that passed failed to notice one small detail.

No doubt the whole episode was overwhelming and quite a spectacle to the witnesses who had gathered. There hung Jesus being crucified as he was being stoned to death. And the sign above his head had riveted and focused all their attention on him. The insults were hurled from the crowd as were the stones, so it was understandable they would not notice that one small detail.

His face was bloodied by the countless stones striking his face. In fact, as he hung there naked, his whole body was struck. He was bloodied, battered, and sliced up by the rocks.

> "His visage was so marred more than any man,
> and his form more than the sons of men"
>
> **(Isa. 52:14)**

It was a spectacle all right. This was a man cursed by God, they thought, just as the law required. It was a gruesome sight.

> "for it is written, cursed is every one that
> hangeth on a tree"
>
> **(Gal. 3:13)**

The purpose of the hanging someone from a tree, according to the law, was to cleanse the land, but was also to send a message. It was a warning.

This is what happens to anyone who commits crimes against God and Israel. This was also a message, namely: "Don't you dare make the same mistake or it will happen to you in like manner." This is what they saw as they passed Jesus, and this was the message. So they didn't notice.

This was the law, and the law was good.

They had to keep their distance, however; or they would have become defiled and unfit for the Passover celebration. But even though they kept their distance and stood back from the horrific sight they still did not notice.

Jesus was crucified somewhere between nine am. and twelve noon. In the milieu they missed it! But it was just a small detail; no big deal. And what is astonishing and kept from the general view over the centuries was that one small little detail that no one seemed to notice.

In fact, even to this day, it has escaped notice; however, in actuality it was no small detail. In fact, it was an *enormous* detail because of its ageless message and its powerful spiritual implication.

As they passed by Jesus, they did not notice that he was hanging from a tree whose roots were sticking up from the ground. It was the fig tree that had withered and had all but died.

It was the very fig tree he had cursed several days earlier. He was hung from the fig tree!

Christ made a massive statement about what he had just accomplished, and it was underscored on the very symbol—the fig tree—which represented the Tree of Knowledge of Good and Evil, which is the law.

Now look at this scripture again, and the meaning is so striking in light of this small detail.

> "having canceled the charge of our legal
> indebtedness [the law], which stood against

us and condemned us; he has taken it away,
nailing it to the cross [patibulum]"

(Col 2:14, NIV)

He was then hung from the tree. What tree? The cursed
fig tree.

But those who passed by hurling stones did not and could
not see. They did not notice the fig tree and neither has it been
noticed down through the centuries. Religious tradition has
prevailed. There has come a misdirected focus away from the
enormous significance of this one small detail.

And when he said, "It is finished" (John 19:30), it was
because the great curse of the law had finally been removed and
done away with.

This was sealed by his crucifixion on the very symbol that
represented that which caused the down- fall of the human race
in the first place. The law, as symbolized by the fig tree, was dead.
He has done away with that which condemns. He underscored
his victory over the law by being slain on the very symbol that
represented the law.

"It is finished"

He died not only to forgive sin, but also to take away the
ordinances that were written against us, and the very power of
sin, which is the law.

Can it be any more obvious and understandable?

Let the celebration begin.

"There is therefore now no condemnation to
them which are in Christ Jesus, who walk not
after the flesh, but after the Spirit. For the law

of the Spirit of life in Christ Jesus hath made
me free from the law of sin and death."

(Rom 8:1–2)

Chapter 24

THE APPLICATION

୬∼ଡ଼

Now consider the impact of this mind picture on our daily lives, and then on our receiving of Holy Communion. When Jesus changed the Passover elements to his own blood (represented by the wine) and body (represented by bread), his message was clear.

> "For I have received of the Lord that which also I delivered unto you, that the Lord Jesus the same night in which he was betrayed took bread: And when he had given thanks, he breaks it, and said, Take, eat: this is my body, which is broken for you: this do in remembrance of me. After the same manner also he took the cup, when he had supped, saying, this cup is the new testament in my blood: this do ye, as

oft as ye drink it, in remembrance of me. For
as often as ye eat this bread, and drink this
cup, ye do shew the Lord's death till he come.
Wherefore whosoever shall eat this bread, and
drink this cup of the Lord, unworthily, shall be
guilty of the body and blood of the Lord"
(1 Cor. 11:23–27)

We are directed to take Communion often. Why? Because
there is a tendency to forget. We go back to sleep.

When Paul wrote to the Galatians about their grave error,
and when he rebuked Peter it was because they were adding
the law to God's free gift of forgiveness and the removal of
the law. Why? Why did they do this? The answer is they felt
unworthy. They felt the need to do something more to assuage
their feeling of unworthiness or guilt. In adding works, they
were demonstrating they had fallen back under the law. The law
Jesus removed.

The temptation to add law to grace is a common problem.
It happens every day to all of God's people. We feel unworthy.
Why do we feel this feeling? The answer is because as we live
out our lives in our body we are still prone to sin.

When a person accepts Jesus as the one who died for their
sins, they fail to recognize they still have to deal with their body
every day. We are still here in the flesh. And this day-to-day
reality is, if I may say so, a chore. This is why we are invoked to
take up our patibulum (not Roman cross) daily—this is a figure
of speech not a literal patibulum obviously.

The body we live in is still sinful. It must be con- trolled.
Not such an easy chore.

"And every man that striveth for the mastery
is temperate in all things"

(1 Cor. 9:25)

"Then said Jesus unto his disciples, if any man
will come after me, let him deny himself, and
take up his [patibulum], and follow me. For
whosoever will save his life shall lose it: and
whosoever will lose his life for my sake shall
find it."

(Matt. 16:24)

Every day we have to walk out our lives dealing with the
body's tendency to sin. So we have two natures, an inner man
and an outer man. Our outer man must be crucified daily, and our
inner man must be renewed. By taking up our patibulum daily,
we are acknowledging this dual reality. When we fail to see this,
we fall under a guilty conscience because our body sins, hence
the feeling of unworthiness floods in again and again. We must
spiritually manage our lives by taking up the patibulum daily.

When we fail to repent after each occurrence of a sin, we
fall into the feeling of unworthiness because we place ourselves
back under the law. Then the common temptation is to try to
adjust ourselves, our conscience, by doing something good. We
try to balance the scale, so to speak, but it is futile.

This was what was happening to Peter and all the others in
Galatia. That is why Paul lamented of the predicament:

"O wretched man that I am! who shall deliver
me from the body of this death?"

(Rom. 7:24)

We must come to grips with the duality of our being. So we take communion to call to mind the Lord's death, but calling to mind his death means we should do this accurately.

He died for the forgiveness of sins, but he died on a fig tree signifying the removal and the end of the law which condemns.

People feel unworthy because they do not have a mental picture of the removal of the law and the condemnation which is caused by the law.

Now we have a vivid mental picture of the law being removed as Jesus hangs from the fig tree. How does being crucified on a pagan cross convey the same power and meaning of being crucified on a fig tree? It doesn't!

And it is not a coincidence that these same religious people try to compensate by doing good deeds in a vain attempt to find favor with God. It is a feeble attempt to adjust their conscience. But all they have to do is look to the fig tree.

There is now no condemnation (nothing that can accuse) because Jesus nailed the law to the fig tree, and in addition, he killed the tree. Now our freedom becomes vividly clear in the chamber of our imagination.

And a person does not have to wait for communion at church to apply the spiritual remedy. The blood of Jesus forgives of sin, but the fig tree conveys they spiritual reality of no condemnation. There is nothing left to judge because there is no longer the law. It has been removed!

In the mercy of God, he does not want us to be miserable and feel unworthy. All one has to do is acknowledge one's sin ask for forgiveness and call to mind the fig tree.

The tree representing both the sacrifice in which Christ's blood was shed and the removal of the law is the perpetual antidote for guilt and the feeling of unworthiness.

The picture of the fig tree is easier to understand as a message then a written doctrine. But the Christian brand of the Roman cross does not convey the image of the law being cursed.

The power of sin is the law that Jesus abolished. It was not a pagan Roman cross on which he died, but a fig tree.

The great tragedy—and irony for those who hold to the pagan Roman cross—is that they still live perpetually under the law. That is why they continually feel unworthy. The fact of the matter is that the brand of Christianity which is represented by the Roman cross does not convey the meaning of the law being taken out of the way. What a tremendous freedom in seeing and knowing there is no judgment for believers.

Only the fig tree and Christ's death on the fig tree gives a true picture of him cursing the law and removing it from condemning. It is not just a symbol, it is a spiritual reality and effect.

What the fig tree means is that judgment day is canceled for those who look upon it. Caution! Having the law removed does not give us license to do whatever we please.

The book of Revelation twenty-two reveals what God thinks about judgment day. There is no fig tree ever again seen, only the Tree of Life.

Just look to the fig tree where Jesus died.

Epilogue

ℛ

D id he or didn't he? Did Nathanael see angels ascending and descending or did he not?

What started with a subtle introduction comes full circle. It started with Nathanael being discovered under the fig tree. It was promised to him that he would see angels ascending and descending on the Son of Man. There is no biblical reference to this promise ever having taken place. Why? Why isn't there?

Such a significant promise, but no biblical record of it having occurred? Did Nathanael ultimately see angels ascending or descending on Jesus or not?

What happened to that promise? Christ said to Nathanael, "you will see angels ascending and descending on the son of man." Nathanael went through this incredible process but never saw the promise of angels ascending and descending on the son of man? If he did there is no recording of the event in the scriptures.

What is going on here? Such a significant promise, but no record of it having occurred? Did Nathanael ultimately see angels ascending or descending on Jesus or not?

Maybe he did but not the way one would commonly think.

Nathanael could have remembered an event in Jewish history where something such as this where angels had ascended and descended. Jacob of old had this special occurrence of angels ascending and descending as he laid sleeping with his head on a rock. But the promise was not about recalling the past it was something that would happen specifically to Nathanael in the future.

Perhaps he did see, but not in the way one would have ever expected. The common assumption is that Jesus was referring exclusively to himself as the "son of man."

Jesus did use this term to describe himself, but the term son of man was also used for other people in the bible as well. In fact, over one hundred times the term son of man appears in the Old Testament. Perhaps the reason we do not see Nathanael in the biblical record witnessing angels ascending and descending on Jesus is because Jesus was not just exclusively referring to himself.

Could it be the promise of angels ascending and descending had a broader application and was to happen upon Nathanael as well? Was Nathanael also to be considered as a son of man? Was it a promise to Nathanael of what would be his own experience? Of course! The promise was in fact all inclusive.

We are all ben Adam [son of man].

The promise of angels ascending and descending on the son of man was not just to Nathanael alone. It is for everyone. Is this your experience? Do you experience angels ascending and descending on yourself ? Sadly, the answer is that this is not the case for most. But, it should be! The major reason it is not is because of the sense of unworthiness that clouds perceptions. But the promise is clear. Look at this scripture which conjuncts with the all-inclusive promise.

> "Are they [angels] not all ministering spirits,
> sent forth to minister for them who shall be
> heirs of salvation?"
>
> **(Heb. 1:14)**

When Jesus went into the temple and threw over the tables He declared, "my Father house is a house of prayer." While there is no longer a physical temple (there will come another physical temple in Jerusalem) we who follow the Lord Jesus are now God's house. Our primary purpose and function on earth is to be a house of prayer.

But many times our prayers are hindered. This is because of two reasons: One we feel unworthy to lift our hearts and heads to pray and so we don't pray at all. And two, if we do manage to lift up prayer Lucifer attacks our prayers. When we are under the law he can accuse us before God. He uses the law as an instrument and grounds for accusations. He argues his case against us when we are using the law to justify ourselves.

We can deal with the first issue by calling to mind and expressing the shedding of Christ blood for our sins. We are forgiven. Secondly, Satan cannot condemn us because he has no grounds. He uses the Law to condemn us, and he uses the law to accuse us before God. But he cannot do that (unless we let him) because the law is gone. He cannot condemn us before God. He cannot legally hinder our prayers.

Angels are messengers. They carry messages. When there comes the message of deliverance from the law, by the cursed fig tree, there is a fresh boldness that attends our confidence. The house of God, which is you, is restored to a house of prayer. Prayers are messages. It is angels who carry these messages into God's presence to be heard. That is why they ascend first. This is hard for people to connect with because it is a spiritual reality. It is not of this world. But it is nonetheless true.

The prayers are carried up to God, and the angels returning are the answers the angels bring back. They ascend and then descend on us. The removal of the fig tree (the law) brings a sense of acceptance. It allows a person to see themselves as worthy. Look on the tree. The is no Law. It is gone. You are worthy because Christ's death made you worthy. All judgement was given by the Father to the Son, and the Son has taken away any judgement, whatsoever, when he took away the law.

> "For the promise, that he should be the heir of
> the world, was not to Abraham, or to his seed,
> through the Law, but through the righteousness
> of faith"
> **(Rom. 4:13)**

There no longer exists or remains any judgment, either from the Father or the Son.

> "When Jesus therefore had received the
> vinegar, he said, it is finished; and he bowed
> his head, and gave up the ghost"
> **(John 19:30)**

We see in the fig tree the absolute completion of Christ's rescue mission.

Welcome to a successful and powerful prayer life. The temple is cleansed, and the law has been removed.

Look on the unforgettable tree.

Endnotes

1. Matthew 3:16–17
2. Numbers 24:17
3. John 1:48
4. Exodus Chapter 11
5. Secrets of Golgotha, Dr. Ernest Martin
6. Ibid pp137–138
7. Matthew 21:1–17; Mark 11:1–11; Luke 19:29–40; John 12:12–19
8. Acts 7:53; Hebrews 2:2; Gal. 3:19
9. Joshua 3:3
10. For a thorough proof of where the former Jewish Temples were actually built, see the film "Jerusalem and the Lost Temple of the Jews" at kenkleinproductions.net
11. Ezekiel 11:23
12. Numbers 19:1–3
13. The Temples that Jerusalem Forgot, Dr. Ernest Martin p 232
14. Matthew 24:1–2

15. Wars of the Jews, Josephus 5.4.1; also "Jerusalem and the Lost Temple of the Jews" (kenkleinproductions.net)

16. Wars of the Jews, Josephus Book 6, Chapter 1; also Matthew 24:1–2

17. 1 Chronicles 29

18. Antiquities Josephus 13.8.3–4

19. Ibid. 17.7.1

20. Nicene and post Nicene fathers, s2.vol 5 (29). p. 804

21. Wars of the Jews Josephus 7.8.6

22. Life of Constantine Euseubius II.55.

23. The 1896 discovery of the Cairo Genizah was one of the greatest Jewish treasures... including commentary on some Mishna tractates and a number of letters.

24. Peter's Jerusalem pp.187–9

25. The Temples that Jerusalem Forgot, Dr. Ernest Martin pp.122-125

26. Ibid. p 232

27. for a more comprehensive presentation please view "Jerusalem the Centre of the Earth" at www.kenkleinuniversity.com

28. "Jerusalem and the Lost Temple of the Jews" (kenkleinproductions.net) Secrets of Golgotha, Dr. Ernest Martin pp 98–99

29. "Jerusalem and the Lost Temple of the Jews" (kenkleinproductions.net)

30. Antiquities of the Jews, XIII. 6, 7 Temples, p. 329

31. "Jerusalem and the Lost Temple of the Jews" (kenkleinproductions.net)

32. Matthew 21:12

33. Secrets of Golgotha, Dr. Ernest Martin pp 98–99

34. Matthew 27:54

35. Secrets of Golgotha, Dr. Ernest Martin

36. http://www.chabad.org/

37. Jeremiah 31:31

38. Leviticus 10–1

39. Deuteronomy 21:20–23

40. In Sanhedrin 43b Babylonian Talmud: Tractate Sanhedrin. Folio 43a

41. as a side note, it was after the Council of Nicaea that Constantine murdered his wife and son
42. Mark 14:49
43. Leviticus 21:18